SHELF LIFE

Thom Gunn was born in Gravesend in 1929. After National Service, he read English at Trinity College, Cambridge, and had his first book of poems, *Fighting Terms*, published while he was still an undergraduate. He moved to North California in 1954 and now teaches half of each year at Berkeley. He was awarded the first FORWARD PRIZE FOR POETRY in 1992 the LENORE MARSHALL POETRY PRIZE in 1993, when he also published his *Collected Poems* and was made a MacARTHUR FELLOW.

THOM GUNN

Shelf Life

Essays, Memoirs and an Interview

faber and faber
LONDON · BOSTON

First published in the United States of America in 1993
by the University of Michigan Press, Ann Arbor
First published in Great Britain in 1994
by Faber and Faber Limited
3 Queen Square London WC1N 3AU

This paperback edition published in 1996

Printed in England by Clays Ltd, St Ives plc

A CIP record of this book
is available from the British Library

ISBN 0-571-17487-6

2 4 6 8 10 9 7 5 3 1

To Clive Wilmer

Contents

I

Enmeshed with Time: The Sixteenth Century   3

Forays against the Republic: Whitman   15

Responsibilities: Contemporary Poetry and
  August Kleinzahler   22

Three Hard Women: H.D., Marianne Moore,
  and Mina Loy   33

What the Slowworm Said: Eliot, Pound,
  and Bunting   53

As If Startled Awake: The Poetry of Janet Lewis   66

Weedy Speech and Tangled Bank:
  Lorine Niedecker   74

Out of the Box: Elizabeth Bishop   77

Small Persistent Difficulties: Robert Creeley   87

Living in the Present: Donald Hall   96

A Record: Allen Ginsberg's Poetry   102

Surefire Diver: Jack Sharpless   116

Fever in the Morning: Jim Powell   121

II. Two Essays on Robert Duncan

The High Road: A Last Collection   129

Adventurous Song: Robert Duncan as
  Romantic Modernist   143

III

Christopher Isherwood: Getting Things Right   173

On a Drying Hill: Yvor Winters   197

Two Saturday Nights: Rewriting a Poem   213

An Anglo-American Poet: Interview with
  Jim Powell   218

I

Enmeshed with Time

The Sixteenth Century

Every now and again, an anthology is published which is also a real book. That is, the editor's selection shows us fresh ways of reading a poetry. Such a work is *The New Oxford Book of Sixteenth Century Verse,* edited by Emrys Jones: it is like a first-class history, only better because it consists of all the data, and we draw the conclusions for ourselves.

The Oxford series of English poetry by the century, which were always a cut above other anthologies, are being reissued volume by volume in new versions, reedited and reconceived. The predecessor of this one, edited by Sir Edmund Chambers in 1932, was not one of the most useful. I have owned a copy since I was an undergraduate forty years ago, and I am grateful for it, as it provided me with the texts of work by poets whose books I couldn't afford to buy. I first read Wyatt in it, for example, and "Orchestra" by Sir John Davies, and a rather bland selection from Greville which was still better than nothing. But Sir Edmund's taste had its limitations. "Elizabethan poetry is characteristically a light-hearted poetry," he stated in his introduction, and though he was forced in all honesty to qualify his view a little, he was obviously happiest when emphasizing the Merrie England, or Hey nonny nonny, aspect of the century: the more shepherds, nightingales singing Jug jug, and pastoral ornamentation the better.

Review of *New Oxford Book of Sixteenth Century Verse,* ed. Emrys Jones (Oxford: Oxford University Press, 1991). Reprinted from *Times Literary Supplement,* August 16, 1991.

In a sense, Emrys Jones's Introduction to the *New Oxford Book of Sixteenth Century Verse* forestalls the reviewer, since it contains the best description possible of both Chambers's editorial assumptions and his own. Pointing out that Chambers's is a prejudice in favor of the "lyric" (ultimately derived from Palgrave, it tends to exclude other kinds of poetry), he wishes to be more inclusive, in particular to take notice of what he calls "the historically circumstantiated." The latter he defines as "poems which enthusiastically embrace the untidy and perhaps obscure specificity of transient historical situations." Thus he healthily disregards both large notions of universality and narrow ones of poetic autonomy, implicitly recognizing that it is the very specialness of a writer's utterance, its enmeshment with temporal circumstances, that produces the literature and in turn evokes the imaginative sympathy and interest of a reader (who is usually as much attracted by unlikeness as by likeness). There is of course more than one kind of history: there is the history of events and politics and social conditions, and there is also the history of developing styles. An example of the first comes early, in the inclusion of extracts from Skelton's "Speak, Parrot," the satire on "the bragging butcher" Wolsey. And stylistic history is both illustrated and clarified by the anonymous account of the battle of Flodden Field (1515), with its still medieval versification. Both kinds of history are relevant to George Cavendish's "Epitaph" on Queen Mary, not a very good poem but an interesting and instructive one, for it demonstrates at the same time the ready identification between the English Queen and the Virgin, and the metrical uncertainty still obtaining in 1559, being written in a hybrid form of alliterative line and rhyming stanza.

Jones presents the marvelous century in a variety so thickly packed that it will have surprises, I imagine, even for those who think themselves well read in it. His formula enables him not only to give us the best poems, but to document the life out of which they came. Poems by recusants and about their executions may serve as a check to the sentimentalized Tudor history of novels like *Fire over England*. There is even one about the burning of an admirably unrepentant atheist (so Marlowe wasn't unique!). The literature of the streets, broadsides and ballads, is mixed in with that of the court, the associates of the gentry, and the university-educated, with which we are more familiar. Among them, George Gascoigne is now represented by his strongest poems (Chambers slighted him dreadfully), Greville by the best of both his love poems and his sonorous Calvinist laments, and even Sidney more widely than ever—by a greater number of sonnets and by some of the experiments with poetic forms. Translations are numerous, as they were in the century itself. The long excerpt from Arthur Golding's *Metamorphoses* reminds me again of how enjoyable it can be when read in selection: to render Morpheus as "Morph" or "Morphy" is merely quaint, but you begin to experience the engrossing power of the verse and the story as you read on, especially if you follow Ezra Pound's advice to read for sense and syntax and not allow the fourteeners to degenerate into a sing-song. As for Marlowe's translations, his Lucan is a contemporary of *Tamburlaine,* and his Ovid is a dandy like the young Donne. Historical circumstantiality, in fact, creates a network of relationships that places everyone more clearly, as we can see with Shakespeare's long poems, which are set firmly in a narrative context of leisurely elaboration and ingenuity.

By avoiding a sharp distinction between the documentary and the literary, Jones also points to some of the originating impulses of poetry. Sixteenth-century people still considered verse a natural medium for the recording of truths, whether practical or moral, whether in the prolixity of Thomas Tusser's *Five Hundred Points of Good Husbandry* (analogous to *Works and Days* or *Old Moore's Almanac*) or more impressively in poor young Chidiock Tichborne's one poem lamenting the pithy paradoxes of his approaching execution. The first being such a hack, and the second being the author of only one poem, I doubt if we would consider either Tusser or Tichborne "a serious poet" nowadays, but for each—all the more in the absence of a succinct and workable prose—poetry was the form answering their need for what Auden called memorable speech. Like the graffiti writer or the composer of an obituary, they had something on their minds that had to be put into words. The pressure to record has always been the starting point of poetry, now as four hundred years ago, and if we disregard the primitive mnemonic urgency that underlies all writing, we do so at our cost. It was particularly visible in a century in which English poetry had to, if not create itself, create itself afresh.

One of the pleasures peculiar to the study of this era is that of seeing the ways in which the various poets made their stylistic choices. The fact that the choices were urgent and seldom clear-cut gives some of the poetry early in this volume its difficult and precarious life—you can still feel the risk involved, for it was a matter of feeling alternatives out, of trying to make the best of two sets of possibilities. For example, there was the choice between the elementary need I've referred to, the desire to record something about crops or the shortness of life, and on the other hand the love of play for its own sake, so that decoration might fill every corner of the poem. But how much play can you introduce without trivializing the subject matter? And how much statement can you insist on without banishing all the fun? There was of course also a metrical choice, as the potential of the iambic line became slowly apparent, and it was often far from obvious for Wyatt, or even for later poets like Cavendish. There was a choice to make between the lengthy medieval discursiveness of, say, Sir Thomas More, and an aphoristic Roman compression. And there was a choice to make between a native style of narration inherited in some way from the Ballads, the material irregularly dramatized and abridged, and the sophisticated battery of devices imported from other literatures, from (for example) Petrarch and Ronsard and Ovid.

Sir Thomas Wyatt, early in the century, is faced with all these choices and more. Not only is he a symptomatic figure but he is emerging, in our own time, as a poet of greater weight and scope than has been heretofore recognized, and so the selection from him may be treated as a test of the editor's method and judgment. Jones shows us a Wyatt new to anthologies, a participant in history and a stylistic colonist claiming land on which will be based many of the great fortunes of the late-century. He is famous already as England's first Petrarchan, true, but his poetry is more varied and ambitious than that: he is defined here not only as the unfortunate and indignant lover of the famous poems, which are properly included, but as the author of all three epistolary satires, of one of the penitential psalms, and of three poems unknown to Chambers.

Wyatt was more than a player in the game of love, he was a successful diplomat and a sometimes successful courtier. The activities were connected, as Stephen Greenblatt has pointed out in his brilliant chapter on Wyatt in *Renaissance Self-Fashioning*. Love was entangled with other kinds of power-game, and Henry VIII's court was a much more dangerous place than a singles bar in San Francisco. Wyatt's poetry at its best often becomes an instrument for examining the assumptions governing conduct in these games, perhaps more searchingly than he intends. Of his most famous poem, "They flee from me," Greenblatt says,

> one is aware . . . of a painful striving toward a perception that remains just beyond the field of vision, an unsettling intimation that the link between male sexuality and power has produced this mingled frustration, anxiety, and contempt.

Wyatt is an expert player but senses in his own consciousness of impoverishment that what has brought him to this pass might not be losing the game so much as playing it at all. The tentativeness and conditionality of the perception hardly diminish its force: it is all the more powerful for being as it were unwilled and unforeseen.

Among the love poems included there are already more notes struck than simply that of rejection by a cruel mistress and the consequent vengeful whining. We have a farewell to love, to compare with so many others of the century; the conjectural "I am as I am" (talk about self-fashioning!); and the poem in which he congratulates himself on being better off with "Phyllis" than with "Brunet that set my wealth [well-being] in such a roar." Jones conjectures that Brunet is Ann Boleyn, and indeed the historical Wyatt barely escaped execution as the Queen's putative lover. Also here, then, are two important poems connected with that story, neither of them published until 1961. I was familiar with one of them, "Who list his wealth and ease retain," with its resonant refrain from Seneca, *circa Regna*

7

tonat, [Jove] thunders round a throne. As in Dunbar's most famous refrain, the authority of the Latin suggests the monumental obduracy of an unyielding truth that makes the English of its application all the more vulnerable—vulnerable to the point of poignancy in the personal instance of the third stanza. Here he refers to what he witnessed through a grating while imprisoned in the Tower:

> The bell tower showed me such sight
> That in my head sticks day and night.
> There did I learn out of a grate
> For all favour, glory, or might
> That yet *circa Regna tonat*.

We may assume that the sight was of Ann's beheading. Autobiographical detail, however discreet and allusive, is given a sudden symbolic force as in Yeats—though the symbol is more proportionate to reality than it ever was for Yeats—after which the return to generalizations of caution in the concluding stanza is all the more moving.

The other recently discovered poem I rejoice to find here, "In mourning wise," I had both read and not read before. That is, I had read the collected edition that included it, but I did not remember reading it, and Jones's singling it out for inclusion is for me one of the great gifts of his anthology. It is related in subject matter to the previous poem, in that it mourns the death of the five with whom the Queen was supposed to have committed adultery, a death that might have been Wyatt's too, but this is less a poem about himself and his fortune than a memorial to them. The range of his feeling is considerable, for he thinks as he grieves. He asserts his right, which some would contest, to lament the deaths of traitors. And he distinguishes between them, telling the reader how each meant something different to him; but in these lines he weeps for all:

> And thus, farewell, each one in hearty wise.
> The axe is home, your heads be in the street.
> The trickling tears doth fall so from mine eyes,
> I scarce may write, my paper is so wet.

The axe's work is over and their heads are on display, but the phrases employed are so mildly, almost *comfortably* familiar that they increase the horror of the line, of which the implication might be that executions have become by now an everyday and homely routine. The understated force is such that it spills over into a kind of authentification of the next two lines, making us read as simple truth an imagery that might otherwise have seemed commonplace in its overstatement.

As I have suggested, the history illustrated by this poetry is stylistic as well as political. Wyatt, at first sight merely the Petrarchan lutanist plaining his sorrows, *thinks* through his poetry. His way of making careful discriminations, whether of emotions or of ideas, influences later poets. As Jones points out in his introduction, he "hands on" to Gascoigne a "special gravity and seriousness," who then hands it on to Ralegh. In the course of his first satire, Wyatt lists the various actions he is too scrupulous to perform: for example, "I cannot wrest the law to fill the coffer," and Gascoigne echoes him in his "Woodmanship," when he speaks of himself in the third person as a mercenary soldier:

> He cannot stoop to take a greedy prey
> Upon his fellows grovelling in the streets.

And what does Ralegh's speaker make in her answer to Marlowe's enraptured Shepherd but worldly-wise discriminations? Just beyond the end of the century and this anthology another ex-mercenary, Ben Jonson, addressing Sir Robert Wroth, will distinguish between him and the soldier who can

> . . . blow up widows, orphans, and their states,
> And think his power doth equal Fate's.

(That is what Sir Robert "cannot" do.) The style of discrimination is similar in each case, largeness of possibility being limited by moral scruples. Accordingly it is a historical pleasure to trace through the century a style that is essentially one of statement, starting with a need to withdraw from experience into a formulation about it so as not to be overwhelmed by it. The ordering of experience, in much of Wyatt, Gascoigne, and Ralegh, therefore becomes itself the experience of the poem.

Pointing to the persistence of the discursive style is not to deny an equal importance to that other famous style which much rather catches the eye in the second, or Elizabethan, part of the century. In "Orchestra," Davies praises Homer for "his abundant verse," and he himself celebrates abundance in both style and subject. Abundance means literally an overflowing, and abundant verse is generous, giving us more than is necessary, even to excess. It takes pride in not discriminating. Speaking of rivers, Davies says later in the same poem:

> Of all their ways, I love Meander's path,
>   Which, to the tunes of dying swans, doth dance;
> Such winding sleights, such turns and tricks he hath,
>   Such creeks, such wrenches, and such dalliance,
>   That, whether it be hap or heedless chance,
>   In his indented course and wriggling play,
>   He seems to dance a perfect cunning hay.

He describes here the very verse he is writing. If the discursive poet is concerned with the serious matter of getting a weight off his chest, with saying something, the poet of abundance is concerned rather with playing. Leisurely and elaborate, his wriggling play often covers as much ground as it can, winding because he enjoys covering it with intricate designs: he includes as much of experience as he can, and I would say he *embellishes* it, if the word did not imply a detachable ornamentation, whereas play is an extension of the imaginative experience itself in such poetry as the above: Meander is what he is only if he meanders. Spenser of course exemplifies this style too, perhaps most perfectly in the wedding poems, in one of which he has as refrain variations on the lines

> And evermore they Hymen, Hymen, sing,
> That all the woods them answer and their echo ring.

In a poem where so much of the musical effect is created by an irregular generosity of rhyme, no image of aural abundance could be more appropriate than that of echo.

I have entered on a familiar precinct of literary history here, one which Jones, probably wisely, avoids in his introduction. He glances at the two dominant Tudor styles but does not label them. Not all critics have been so guarded: C. S. Lewis called them Drab and Golden; Yvor Winters Plain and Ornate; and others have given them other names. In describing them as the poetries of discrimination and abundance I am trying to recognize that the styles are not always or necessarily in mutual opposition. Now they may be distinct, but now they may be continuous one with the other. Wyatt's "In mourning wise" or Greville's "Down in the Depths" may define one extreme of the century's styles (not at all drab, and not that plain either) and Spenser's "Epithalamion" or Davies's "Orchestra" the other (certainly both golden *and* ornate), but they may turn out to be merely the outer edges of a single discourse, not incompatible with one another any more than our sensations need be incompatible with our minds. The styles are to be found together inside single poems like Drayton's "Since there's no help" or Greville's "All my senses." Davies is abundant in some of his poetry, discriminatory to the point of harshness elsewhere. Both modes are available to all of the later Elizabethans, to the song-writers as much as to the composers of longer works. That is perhaps what makes for the largeness of scope in the poets at the end of the century and the beginning of the next, where the poets often move between the styles or combine them without any sense of discrepancy. There is thus a weight to the achievement of such individual poems as Campion's best songs or Nashe's plague poems that makes it difficult to call them "minor," even when you compare them with the best, with Shakespeare, Marlowe, Donne, or Jonson, unless by minor you are referring merely to bulk of written work.

> If all would lead their lives in love like me,
> Then bloody swords and armour should not be;
> No drum nor trumpet peaceful sleeps should move,
> Unless alarm came from the camp of Love.

This is, of course, merely a conceit, we may say, and one paraphrased from Propertius at that. But to speak so is to overlook the wonderful boldness with which Campion plunges into his wild assertion (wild, but completely reasonable) at the same time that every detail of the sound is exquisitely regulated. Abundance is not quenched here, nor is the power of discrimination. Rather, in the triumph of combining the utmost polish with the utmost exuberance, Campion has achieved a fresh synthesis of the two, one of many that come at the end of the century. There is no question of "a tough reasonableness beneath the slight lyric grace"—the lyric grace itself was tough, and reasonableness had never been alien to it. Neither the power of thought nor the ability to enjoy the world is suspended for an instant in the song from which these lines are taken.

In his introduction to the old anthology, apropos of *The Shepherd's Calendar*, Chambers remarked heartily: "And thereafter, of course, there is God's plenty." Nevertheless, the last phase of the century presents a problem to the anthologist who must end his work at 1600, for that year arbitrarily cuts in half the great period of poetry most easily defined as being between 1580 and 1620. The problem is compounded by our inability to date Shakespeare's *Sonnets,* Donne's love poems, Greville's *Caelica,* or many other works of the time, other than approximately. Both editors claim the whole of Shakespeare, but otherwise Jones deals with the question in a completely different way from Chambers, and I must say I prefer his solution, which emphasizes the variety rather than the supposed unity of Elizabethan poetry. For example, he claims all of Greville, whose religious poetry Chambers excluded. More crucially, Chambers left Donne to the seventeenth century, as did many other anthologists and critics, so that I grew up with the distinct impression that Donne was a later poet than he really was, a successor to Shakespeare and even a kind of contemporary to Marvell. Yet he seems to have started writing at about the same time as Shakespeare, "The Storm" and "The Calm" are clearly dated by their occasion, the Azores expedition of 1597, and most of his Elegies relate to the same Ovidian fashion as Marlowe's translations of the *Amores*. Moreover, as Jones tells us, "the verse satire of the 1590s which Donne pioneered and of which he was by far the most distin-

guished exponent was exclusively an Elizabethan phenomenon." So he restores Donne's early poetry to its rightful time,
where it is completely at home beside the satires and epigrams
of the 1590s, which Jones is wise enough to include. The
decade is no longer located largely in Arcadia and the Forest
of Arden; it shares them now with the Inns of Court and the
plaguey streets of London.

This *Oxford Book,* with its poems both historically circumstantiated and uncircumstantiated, is more complex and varied and interesting than Chambers ever allowed his to be. I
wouldn't consider it either easy or desirable to read most anthologies straight through, but that's what I did to this, with
an intensifying excitement, recognizing this and that, making
constant happy discoveries, finding certain of my assumptions
confirmed and others overturned—in fact never bored. Jones
has taken the century apart and then, poem by poem, put it
together again so that the canon is permanently extended. It
is largely a matter of accumulating detail, and would be best
summarized by the contents pages. Instead, let me give two
examples of what I called my happy discoveries, the kind of
things that make his selection so lively and fresh. Robert
Southwell, in a poem about the execution of Mary Queen of
Scots, which transformed her, as he says, from Queen to Saint,
from Mary to Martyr, uses the following conceit: "The bud
was opened to let out the rose." It is a clever, bloody, and
beautiful image, making me realize that here is a poet I had
too long taken on trust and ought to read in bulk. The other
example is from George Gascoigne's lines predicting the
spendthrift's future: thou wilt go on, he says,

> Till Davy Debit in thy parlour stand,
> And bids thee welcome to thine own decay.

The bailiff enters the poem with a particularly ominous energy. Both his and Southwell's poems are so good that they
should be better known. Perhaps they will now. And in the
whole book I can think of only two poems whose omission I
regret: Boyd's sonnet "Fra bank to bank" (perhaps because it
is Scots rather than English?) and Campion's "Now winter

nights enlarge." I mention these, not to carp at a great editor, but on the contrary—how often have you come across an anthology in which you miss only two of your favorites? This is a volume, then, that being both inclusive and interpretive may be equally read for pleasure or required as a textbook. And such are its virtues that it might well be used as a handbook in styles by the beginning poet: if studied properly, it would form quite an education.

It is, in short, a necessary anthology. We must give Emrys Jones credit for it now, because in a few years time the fineness of his taste, the range of his research, and the decisiveness of his choices will have become obscured by imitation. So many other anthologies will be influenced by this one that eventually his achievement will seem merely obvious. But it is not, and this is a book for which we should express gratitude.

Forays against the Republic
Whitman

The commentators on Whitman's "Song of Myself" notoriously disagree about its structure. They all feel that the work holds together, but how? It is fascinating to see how little their descriptions of its overall organization have in common. Robert Creeley, at any rate, would not be surprised: he has told an anecdote about a teacher asking graduate students to produce thematic outlines of the poem—and no two of them were the same. Creeley therefore claims Whitman as his own precursor, composing "in a 'field' of activity" rather than according to logical or narrative norms.

Whitman might well have understood, in old age having said of his entire collected poetry: "I consider [it] and its theory experimental—as, in the deepest sense, I consider our American republic itself to be, with its theory." Developing book and developing country, each creates itself as it goes along, realizing itself through its very continued activity, edition by edition.

The initiation and unstopped bubbling source appears to have been "Song of Myself," and a large part of the character of that experiment sprang from the concept of "myself," so different from the first person of Wordsworth's recently published *Prelude* (1850; "Song of Myself" was 1855). Whitman's self is both exceptional and average, representative and individual, a rich young lady and Walt Whitman, one of the

First appeared, in slightly different form, as "Freedom for All," *Times Literary Supplement,* January 5–11, 1990.

roughs and Jesus Christ. Each merges into the other, like leaves of grass into the prairie or individuals into a visionary democracy. A democracy is supposed to be a society of free association, as opposed to one in which there is hierarchical subordination. Thus the poem proceeds in a loosely associationistic manner, its very structure promiscuous and democratic, and Whitman transforms the early Romantic practice of a rather mild associationism into an assured and extreme narrative disjunctiveness that we must look forward some sixty years to equal.

Written, then, with an almost modernist trust in juxtaposition and improvisation, and in the continuing heat of a revelatory experience from 1853, the rich and complex work still has an originality difficult to describe—and not only in its structure. First of all, its free verse, whatever its antecedents, is an invention of great flexibility. It ranges from the anaphoric patterns learned out of the Authorised Version, through a serviceable prosiness, through a mid-Victorian anapestic jig, to the bold nonce rhythms of "How the flukes splash!" and of the following lines:

> Here and there with dimes on the eyes walking,
> To feed the greed of the belly the brains liberally spooning,
> Tickets buying, taking, selling, but in to the feast never once
>   going . . .

Though these tend toward the trochaic, they do not stay quite long enough with it to make it a norm. Nor is the originality of these lines only rhythmical. The imagery has a kind of prelapsarian freshness, boldness, and directness, even while describing such obvious postlapsarians as the midcentury achievers. The vigor of Whitman's observation matches the vigor of what he observes, as if he has only to name it to bring it to life. In "This Compost" (1856), he writes "Out of its little hill faithfully rise the potato's dark green leaves" (Lawrence sounds like this in "Trees in the Garden"). And in the course of another early poem, "To Think of Time," he describes a stage-driver's funeral, and treats the cant phrases of the driver's daily life ("somebody loafing on you, you loafing on somebody headway, man before and man behind") as if they were *things,* as defined and physical in reference as the names of apron, cape, gloves, and whip that they are mixed in with during his account. To these distinctions of overall structure, verse-line, imagery, and language may be added that of the rhetoric itself, the unique approach taken by his whole art of persuasion—so that summing it up in Alastair Fowler's phrase, "Victorian sententiousness," seems inadequate; much more useful is W. S. Di Piero's passing remark that it "is first of all revelatory, often interpretive, seldom explanatory."

The basic revelation seems to have something to do with the sense of a democracy so generous that there is room in it for everyone and everything. For me one of the most moving parts of "Song of Myself" is the passage in which Whitman speaks for the inarticulate and the unheard, for the "deform'd, trivial, flat, foolish, despised, / Fog in the air, beetles rolling balls of dung"—that is, for those who lack even self-definition and for the lowest of the low. Such a revelation is religious in ultimate purport, but his religious feelings are connected with all his other feelings, not only with the political but with the sexual too (which overlap, in their turn). In the words of 1855, later modified several times, he tells us of a hot night with God:

> . . . God comes a loving bedfellow and sleeps at my side all
>   night and close on the peep of the day
> And leaves for me baskets covered with white towels bulging
>   the house with their plenty.

The baskets contain rising dough, of course. Critics refer to them variously as "pregnant," "an allusion to communion baskets," to male naked bellies, to the mother's breasts, and to male erections. But the significance of bread is proverbial, and surely the emphasis here is both more obvious and more irrational than those proposed. Lewis Hyde, with a better sense of proportion than the others, reads the second line most helpfully, stressing the *free gift* of what nourishes the soul as well as the body. The stylistic analogy to be made is with the imagery of the New Testament: "What man is there of you, to whom if his son ask bread, will he give him a stone?" Which writing is also, as Di Piero would say, revelatory but not explanatory.

Of Whitman at his best—that is, "Song of Myself" and some other poems of the 1850s and a few later poems—it is not enough, then, to call the tone sententious. It leans, rather, toward the dramatic (it is seldom far from the spoken voice), and does so most pointedly at the transitions between section and section, because they are those of one uncertain where his drifting consciousness has brought him. "I talk wildly, I have lost my wits," he exclaims, or "Somehow I have been stunn'd." He is often disoriented, not sure where or even who he is, speaking with surprise, bewilderment, or wonder. The transitions are, in fact, like those of dreams, and Robert K. Martin justifiably classes not only "The Sleepers" but "Song of Myself" among the "dream-vision poems."

Such openness to the irrational associations of the unconscious seems to have freed Whitman's imagination into some of the most energetic writing of his early work. I am thinking less of the "ladled cups" of the waves in "Crossing Brooklyn Ferry" than of the later-omitted passages from "The Sleepers" which have properly become so famous in the last few decades. In the longer of these, the dreamer as young woman with and without her lover is abruptly replaced by a presumably male dreamer who finds himself in the street naked ("my clothes were stolen while I was abed"). In his nightmare he regresses to the infant of polymorphous appetite, an appetite both convivial and erotic in its fantasy, where clarity and sharpness of image only accentuate the sense of confusion.

> The cloth laps a first sweet eating and drinking,
> Laps life-swelling yolks . . . laps ear of rose-corn, milky and
>   just ripened:
> The white teeth stay, and the boss-tooth advances in dark-
>   ness,
> And liquor is spilled on lips and bosoms by touching glasses,
>   and the best liquor afterward . . .

The cloth, I think, doubles for both the bedclothes and the table-napkin around the speaker's neck; and "laps" has maybe a primary sense of "wraps around," but with several ancillary senses. Rimbaud would have been interested in this writing, in the way the imagination is freed from traditional restraints—almost but not quite into the meaningless.

But in emphasizing Whitman's experimental originality I should point out that he could also make resourceful use of the rhetoric he found available. He concludes "Crossing Brooklyn Ferry" with a series of apostrophes to a mainly non-human world, of a tiresome sort with which readers had already been long familiar. ("Roll on, thou deep and dark blue ocean—roll!") Whitman gives the device a new function. By granting the river, clouds, foundries, etc., permission, as it were, to be what they are, he is also granting himself permission to be what *he* is—a man, specifically in this poem, promiscuously attracted by other men, and brimming with a mixture of guilt and joy about it.

For at the basis of the basic revelation—that of an ideally generous democracy—is to be found what may be its source, that point already alluded to at which the public and political intersect with the private and sexual. His vision of democracy seems to originate from what you might call a populist taste in men. Though he insists "I am the poet of the woman the same as the man," though he wants to write equally about both sexes from sheer *fairness* as well as from a sense of duty, though it was his acceptance of unabashed female sexuality that most shocked his contemporaries, it is clear ultimately that he loves humanity so much because he loves hunky working men. This is not to call him a hypocrite, for his sympathies do indeed extend to "the snag-tooth'd hostler with red hair," to dwarfs and to the deformed, but it is to point out what seems to have started off and continued to vivify those sympathies. Watching firemen march in a parade, Whitman notices "the play of masculine muscle through clean-setting trowsers and waist-straps," a line in "I Sing the Body Electric" which I have always found especially revealing (though it is probably as revealing of me that I should have noticed it). He likes a body that is at the same time "athletic" in development and "negligent" in attitudes, two favorite words. And they are words that carry a political charge for him as well: for he constantly refers to an athletic democracy, and "negligence" in context suggests generosity carried to the point of carelessness.

There is a contradiction, though, which he is seldom ready to acknowledge. However many partners he may find among the drivers, conductors, delivery boys, milkmen, sailors, and soldiers who carry out the business of the republic, loving them sexually was still an act subversive to the authority of that republic. The contradiction surfaces in one of the "Calamus" poems, like most of them rather thinly written, "We Two Boys Together Clinging." This is a nine-line poem about a pair of life-long lovers, outlaws, "up and down the roads going" of the United States, of which the last line reads "Fulfilling our foray." The foray is against the republic itself: an explicit conflict surfaces, here at least, between the populist athletic democracy and the specific athletic lovers.

We are sometimes tempted to see Whitman only as the ebullient celebrator of an idealized democracy, as if his whole career was of a piece with its initiation. But much of that lengthy experiment consisted of revisions, changes of mind, and silences. It ended, you might say, in prose. And further, if we read carefully enough, we may see that he had always been troubled by inconsistency and conflict, had endured nightmares, and had recurred often to the "terrible doubt of appearances."

Certainly, we primarily value, and will continue to value, the way Whitman extends the defiant admiration of impulse learned from the early Romantics and makes it his own. What poet is more generous? He looks to liberation not merely for the educated, for the noble loners, but for all of us.

> Unscrew the locks from the doors!
> Unscrew the doors themselves from their jambs!

is an extraordinary utterance for 1855, and it was still fresh enough in 1955 for Ginsberg to use it as an epigraph for *Howl and Other Poems*. But to study Whitman is to find how precarious the ebullience always was, and how willed it was to become. What makes the documentary labors of such recent critics as Betsy Erkkila and M. Jimmie Killingsworth useful to us is that they detail the confusions out of which it arises, and show how easily the great gesture dissipated into confusion again: they are helping to demonstrate the full complexity and richness and rareness of what seems, at first hearing, so simple.

Responsibilities

Contemporary Poetry and August Kleinzahler

Helen Vendler starts her anthology with an Introduction phrased in lofty terms. With "a successful poem," she says, "a reader enters and joins—like Keats's spectator of the urn—the procession of forms that give access to an imagined plane of projected existence." The rest of the Introduction is similar in style: it is high-minded and imprecise where the reader would welcome a practical summary of the tendencies at work in poetry since World War II, or perhaps an explanation of her inclusions and exclusions in this book, since many of them are not to be assented to as a matter of course. She does, however, offer an explanation of her reasons for beginning the anthology proper with Wallace Stevens. To initiate an enterprise like this with a forerunner, as a kind of patron saint to what follows, is an established procedure—I recall Yeats starting the first *Oxford Book of Modern Verse* with Pater, or Michael Roberts starting his *Faber Book of Modern Verse* with Hopkins; but since Stevens has not been that pervasive an influence today, or even yesterday, I was curious about her reasons. She acknowledges that Williams and Pound have been important for postwar poetry (how could she not?), but tells us that she chooses Stevens rather than them as "chief link" between us

Review of *Harvard Book of Contemporary Poetry*, ed. Helen Vendler (Cambridge: Harvard University Press, 1985), and *Storm over Hackensack*, by August Kleinzahler (Mt. Kisco, N.Y.: Moyer Bell, 1985). Reprinted from *Threepenny Review* 25 (Spring 1986) and from *PN Review* 55 (1987).

and the Modernists because he took as "total subject" a "cultural skepticism" about the very nature of "perception and memory." Well, yes . . . and again, no: I hesitate in the same way as I did after reading her bit about Keats. *Is* it this subject matter that really distinguishes the poetry of our period? The thought here is elusive because so vague.

We may get a better preview of what is going on by looking at the list of contributors. The four poets chronologically following Stevens are Langston Hughes, Theodore Roethke, Elizabeth Bishop, and Robert Hayden, who make up a group remarkable for its exclusions. On the one hand, no Charles Olson; on the other, no J. V. Cunningham. It is at this point that I begin, uneasily, to understand the nature of this anthology, from which two of the most important lines of tradition in contemporary poetry are to be left out—two lines, it is true, that contradict each other fiercely, but that contain much of the most vigorously alive writing of the last few decades. You could call them the Open and the Closed.

In her Introduction, Vendler says (with almost excessive care) that "resounding closure . . . no longer seems 'true.'" But it turns out that this is a mere bow to current critical jargon, and has nothing to do with the actual content of her anthology. Olson—the poet who actually *feared* closure, the poet who explained to Pound and Williams what they had almost inadvertently done, who in any case mediated between them and the future, the poet of fluidity itself, who in practice flowed like a great excessive and wasteful river all over the surrounding terrain—is unrepresented and nowhere mentioned. Vendler presumably thinks him unimportant.

And the true opposition, the poet any one of whose epigrams would throw Vendler's modish remark back in her teeth—Cunningham, who saw language as the mark of human choice, each phrase a closure, each rhyme an exclusion, who wrote not from idealistic optimism but from the pessimism of experience, "whose poems [were] as well made as wristwatches" (Guy Davenport) yet savagely human in their wit and concentrated passion—he too is unrepresented, though he is also just as much of the period covered by the anthology.

She does not include either of these poets or anybody associated with them. What is left? She seems to have a liking for what I could call the poetry of anxious urbanity, which I understandably connect with the pages of the *New Yorker* (since so much of it originally appeared in them) and of which Bishop and Merrill are the better practitioners. It is no surprise, either, after her studies of them, that she is generous to the delicate irrationalism of a Charles Wright or an Ashbery. And she is a sucker for what M. L. Rosenthal called confessional poetry—Sexton, Plath, Berryman, the lot.

But almost as if to plead that her grounds for choice are not that narrow after all ("Look, I do have other sympathies!"), she prints thirty-six pages of Ginsberg, thus giving him the longest selection here. He is our one genuinely populist poet, and certainly in his directness and energy does a little to counter the massive gentility of the Vendler canon of contemporary verse—but these pages, added to a grudging five of Snyder and nine of O'Hara, are not enough to make up for her notable omissions from the Open writers, even as the inclusion of Robert Pinsky is not enough (though apparently she thinks it is) to make up for her omissions from the Closed.

You can get a good enough idea of what she does include from a specific poet by looking at her selection from Lowell, who is obviously central to our period in many ways, even if sometimes I cannot help wishing he wasn't. It starts with one poem from the books before *Life Studies*, four from that book, and the handsome "Waking Early Sunday Morning" (which is beginning to look like Lowell's best single poem). The remaining nine pages are devoted to sixteen poems from the later poetry, the poetry written out of lithium, the greater deadener of emotion, poetry pathetic in its talkiness and flatness and its desperate amassing of detail for its own sake. She ends with his limp and sketchy "Epilogue," doing a disservice to Lowell by calling it (in her Introduction) "great."

The defects in her selection from Lowell's work are the same as those in her selection of the poets themselves. It seems to me that Vendler's taste and her historical sense are both defective, the two being connected. The result is an anthology more narrowly personal than representative of our period, rather as if someone bringing out a collection of poets with similar retrospective intentions in 1840 should have included heaps of Campbell, Southey, and Tom Moore and completely overlooked Shelley and Landor. It is surely ridiculous that she gives us Amy Clampitt and not Robert Duncan, who is her most serious omission of all, the only living American who might be said to deserve our glibly used encomium of "great." Perhaps after all it is as well for Vendler that she doesn't include him—the presence of his vigor and ambitious imagination would burst the binding of her meanly conceived collection.

My reader may ask at this point why I am so exercised over an obviously worthless book like this. I am because anthologies nowadays are influential. Teachers use them as textbooks, and many teachers use them uncritically, and so we are going to find class after class taught that poor pretentious Amy Clampitt is the real thing while knowing nothing of Duncan or Creeley or Cunningham or Bowers. And I am afraid that this anthology will be so used, because it is edited by the most powerful and widely read poetry critic in the United States (except perhaps Hugh Kenner, who has far wider sympathies), and so the definitions of contemporary poetry thus made will influence the way in which an extensive public defines it. People will, alas, start taking Lowell's "Epilogue" as a poem to study and emulate because Helen Vendler has called it great.

There are better books around if you really need a selective guide to poetry of the last forty years: Donald Hall's *Contemporary American Poetry* (Penguin, second edition), though twenty years old, is shorter but much more balanced; and the latter half of Hayden Carruth's *The Voice That Is Great Within Us* (Bantam, 1970) gives a large and fair sampling of poetry from our period. Both of these need bringing up to date, but either is preferable to Vendler's book. Hall speaks in his crisply written Introduction about the need for "all possibilities" in poetry, "even contradictory ones, to exist together." That is well said, because that need still continues, and I am doubtful that Vendler recognizes it.

In our attempt to determine the patterns to which we ourselves contribute, probably the least difficult part is to talk about the effect of great predecessors. Their careers can be seen as wholes; their estates have been carved up. Thus it is easy to grant that Stevens has been of *some* influence on subsequent American poetry, particularly that written on the Eastern seaboard; and it is equally easy to point out that the examples of Pound and the late Williams initiated a tradition in which poets find possibilities continually more attractive, anarchically explosive as they are to the whole "English" tradition. But the overwhelming influence on American poetry since 1960 has been that of the earlier Williams—the Williams, that is, before *Paterson*. In our versification and subject matter it is evidenced specifically by a preference for the short run-on free-verse line and an insistence on the particulars of everyday life (not on history or philosophy). Williams wrote like this as early as 1917:

> At ten A.M. the young housewife
> moves about in negligée behind
> the wooden walls of her husband's house.
> I pass solitary in my car.
>
> Then again she comes to the curb
> to call the ice-man, fish-man, and stands
> shy, uncorseted, tucking in
> stray ends of hair, and I compare her
> to a fallen leaf . . .

Perhaps he makes that comparison because he recalls Pound's "Liu Ch'e," who when dead became no more than "a wet leaf that clings to the threshold." But for Williams, in any case, it seemed quite natural to think of the uncorseted housewife and the fallen leaf with the same emotion, because of his habitual tenderness toward all that was both vulnerable and ordinary. It is the *feeling* that gives the motivating force to the poem this comes from, in the same way as it does to one of Wordsworth's poems. The kind of language used, the versification, etc., are subordinate to it, and in some sense serve it. And though more recent poets have made easy work of copying the Williams metric, and of writing as if there were no ideas but in things, they have not so easily brought to that metric and those things the rhythms of tenderness or indignation that made them agile and memorable. So you can open almost any American poetry periodical nowadays and find a lot of dead Williams. Dead Williams is just about the same as dead Keats or dead Hopkins—subject dead, language dead, rhythms dead, nothing alive but the ego of the perpetrator.

But for those of talent, the belated influence of this poetry written in the first decades of the century was liberating, and perhaps still is—liberating in many different ways: you can see, for example, how Williams helped Denise Levertov to the lovely fluidity of movement and perception in her early work; or you can equally see how the style of Williams has led a much younger poet, August Kleinzahler, to a kind of poetry making a complete contrast to Levertov's.

Perhaps with Kleinzahler, who was born in New Jersey, the influence came as part of the territory. His first full-length book is called *Storm over Hackensack*, which would seem to allude to his origins with a certain pointedness, if not defiance. And indeed he can afford to be frank in the allusion, because they are just origins—that is, a place to be originated from but not confined in. Kleinzahler has travelled a bit, and his poems are located wherever he has spent time: from Fort Lee and New York he went to Montreal and Vancouver and San Francisco. The poetry of Williams is similarly a point of origin from which he moves out.

I would like to briefly trace this moving-out. A poem called "Real Hair" consists entirely of a barber's speech to his long-haired young customer, and very funny it is too: its apostrophe'd and phonetically rendered dialect could well be by a modern Mark Twain if it were written as prose, but it was Williams, above all, who taught us the effect of such speech when isolated as a poem. At first sight "November in West New York" is similar: a roofer looks out of his window and longs for bad weather while he plays idly with a switchblade someone has given him. It continues:

> The street's three maples
> are nearly stripped
> of the yellow flecking tenement brick
> but no storm yet.
> Just a soft slow afternoon
> on 52nd street.
>
> He's waiting on the storm
> and two fat bids.
> —*One good fucking storm*
> *with lots of wind.*
> *And hail.*
> *And destruction,* he says
>
> flipping that blade,
> waiting for the phone to ring.

Kleinzahler has learned from the proper Imagist precepts: the street is presented physically and concisely, with great sensory force. The passage consists of "writing thoroughly local in origin," it is in a firmly accented and alert free verse, and it is moved by a keen *sympathy* for the roofer. The feeling is not at all the tenderness of Williams for his young housewife or for *his* roofers (in "Fine Work With Pitch and Copper"), because what Kleinzahler delights in is the way that the roofer makes fun of himself, both expressing and dealing with his desire for violence by playing with it, turning it into a comic hyperbole. You can find this sense of violence throughout the book, but it does not roam at large, for it is always countered by his sense of the ridiculous. "Go back to your febrile / needle-work" he says to (presumably) a lover, in another poem, in the midst of righteous scorn breaking up in laughter, as it were, at his own exaggeration of epithet. By exaggerating to the point of fantasy, he makes the violence manageable, turning it on itself. Does this triumvirate of comedy, fantasy, and violence sound like James Tate? Well, it doesn't when you get down to reading the poems themselves instead of my description of them. Kleinzahler is not interested in high jinks for their own sake: joker though he may be, he stays immensely and responsibly on the side of his subject matter. That's a real roofer with a real need for money, after all.

The responsibility also differentiates Kleinzahler from the poet as ordinary guy on the street, that persona which has turned out to be the most depressing consequence of the Williams influence. He may enjoy the locutions of the barber and the roofer, he may very well share them, but he does not subscribe to the anti-intellectualism of the poet writing in the *American Book Review* who claimed that his ten years in a factory were the only proper apprenticeship to poetry. To be a poet you have to be both ordinary *and* extraordinary. Kleinzahler's language in "Show Business," which appears to be a burlesque of erotic fantasy, is as poised and considered as that of Henry James, who also was of course interested in the *spoken* above all. "But God were you ever a Sireen," says the poem to the object of passion, and then records an unforgettable glimpse of her

> on your way out of the Butcher's
> with half a roast and some mustard
> under your arm turning suddenly
> with that look of sexual malice . . .

Such rich and flexible comedy reminds me, for a moment, more of *The Awkward Age* than of *Spring and All*.

In "Indian Summer Night: The Haight," his imagination works upon a more literally autobiographical experience: first he gives us the sounds he can hear in his San Francisco room coming from outside across a small park—the bus, a stand-up comic in a nearby café, street people—and then he recalls how

> The summer my sister worked at Palisades Park
> I'd stay awake till midnight,
> listening.
> When the breeze in the maples was right
> you could hear her

> my sister,
> over the loudspeaker a quarter mile away
> telling the barkers patrons and freaks,
> everybody,
> the last voice before the lights went out,
>
> *—Thank you. Good night.*

Apparently he has no fashionable worries about the reliability of his perceptions in the first half of the poem, nor of his memory in the half I have quoted. Part of the point to what he is telling us, in fact, is that the mind, brain cells still intact, *can* trust itself and its memory. The very structure of the poem is based on such trust, which is symptomatic of the matter-of-fact good health that pervades the whole book: and the structure is a simple and common one, which has been used a thousand times before and will be used a thousand times again: "I notice this now, and it reminds me of something in the past." Its *shape* being so familiar, the poem's power has to rise from the vividness of the performance. The vividness, the bringing to life is of course more than a matter of mere image and vocabulary, the latter of which is here plain to the point of baldness—it must spring from the total effect of the language and rhythms. When you read the whole poem aloud, you notice how, for example, the short lines are important to it for their interrupting effect, which acts both as qualification and as dramatization of the kind of pause it is necessary to make in the careful recalling of a memory. And the details actually recalled bear a complicated relationship—neither of simple contrast nor of simple likeness—to the details earlier in the poem, in which the stand-up comic was speaking to his audience through a mike (a sort of loudspeaker), and in which one at least of the street people, who has "an unwholesome laugh," can be called in the context a different kind of "freak," "Good night" serves as a closure not only to both perception and memory, but also to a poem which has through its instances acted as a moving comment on the passage of time and on listeners at night. It stops short of *overt* comment, but the associations are put together in such a way that it is hardly necessary to do more.

The structure to most of Kleinzahler's poems is rudimentary as a matter of course, because he wants the real poetic work to be performed by the aroused energy of his consciousness acting within it unimpeded. He leads us forward, suggesting, constructing, creating hypotheses (usually in the form of images), until we end with an accumulation of language that is striking, absolutely clear, and yet fully responsible to the richness and complexity of the life which is his subject matter. Thus I return to my idea of his responsibility, but it is a responsibility neither solemn nor stringent, for it results almost always from affection for what he is writing about, which he doesn't want to falsify by omission or evasion.

The example of his art at its highest is to be found in the first poem in the book, "Where Souls Go," which starts as a playful speculation about the afterlife,

> No telling where: down the hill
> and out of sight—
> soapbox derby heroes in a new dimension.

Later, though, he sees that the imagination of such an active existence is an attempt to impose the imagery of the living upon the dead. "Rather," he says of the dead souls, "imagine them in the eaves"

> among pigeons
> or clustered 'round the D-Train's fan
> as we cross the bridge to Brooklyn.
> And make that a Friday night
> July say. We are walking past
> the liquor store to visit our love.
> Two black boys are eating Corn Doodles
> in the most flamboyant ma. ner possible.
> She waits, trying
> to have the best song on as we arrive.
> The moon is blurred.
> Our helicopters are shooting at fieldworkers.
> The Mets are down 3–1 in the 6th.

And that's where it ends. The dead have become torpid, present perhaps but not to be counted among the things that affect what we *do*—what we do, in fact, suddenly taking over the whole poem with great cocky vigor. Once the D-train is mentioned, the dead are apparently forgotten. The details are sketched in quickly but without intensity: it's the sum of them that matters, and the intensity is implied rather than stated in the way that "our" date, an ostensibly trivial event, completely replaces the concern with the afterlife. This, he says, is what matters for the healthy and alive. We can't help it. And yet—the charm of the situation is suddenly put at something of a distance by the last three details, each an item on its separate line. They do not really add up, nor are they meant to, because, I think, they cannot to those caught up in the present and the personal instance. And when we do try to step back, and we juxtapose larger public events (the weather, our colonial wars, sports in the newspapers), we do so without making sense of them, just as we cannot make sense of the dead. The balance Kleinzahler achieves here in his presentation of human delight that is also human triviality, his romantic sympathy and his hard-headedness, the sense of proportion that finally wins out in this excellent poem—these are what I am referring to when I use the word responsibility. But from the start the responsibility takes its origin in an exuberance that both complicates the poetry and makes it worth while. The poetry, need I say, is no longer like that of Williams: here and elsewhere in the book it becomes something new, something perhaps inconceivable to the reader of the Vendler anthology.

Three Hard Women

H.D., Marianne Moore, and Mina Loy

1

A collected poems is a monument, and it often gives you little sense of its author's early poetry, of the ways it seemed fresh, unprecedented, even outrageous, to its first readers. You would be hard put to guess what the *Lyrical Ballads* or the 1855 *Leaves of Grass* were like from Wordsworth's or Whitman's collected works, in which they have become scattered limbs. Redistribution and revision have made the originals hard to reconstruct.

I am concerned in this essay with some twentieth-century poets. Yeats, Marianne Moore, and Auden are merely the most famous of those who suppressed some of their early poetry and altered much of the rest out of all recognition. But the attempt to read a poet's early work for itself and not as part of a career meets more subtle obstacles among other modernists, in whose work such large changes of style took place, for here the obstacles may rather be in the reader's mind. Though *Prufrock* and *Harmonium* are printed as intact units at the start of the collected Eliot and the collected Stevens, you have to make an effort to see them as such, to separate the brilliant self-willed cleverness of the younger men from the sobered meditations that came afterwards. You

Reprinted from *On Modern Poetry: Essays Presented to Donald Davie*, ed. Vereen Bell and Laurence Lerner (Nashville: Vanderbilt University Press, 1988).

tend to keep the latter in mind without meaning to, their weight anachronistically ballasting the early work. Nevertheless, whether the obstacles are outside or inside your mind, it is still worth trying to overcome them in order to read those first books for what they were at the time of publication.

For what they were. Asked in old age about her criteria in selecting material for the *Dial,* Marianne Moore said:

> I think that individuality was the great thing. We were not conforming to anything. We certainly didn't have a policy, except I remember hearing the word "intensity" very often. A thing must have "intensity." That seemed to be the criterion.[1]

The words may sound moderate enough, but the individuality, nonconformity, and intensity she is speaking about are those of, among others, Gertrude Stein, e.e. cummings, Williams, and Stevens, all of whom she admired. However we may see it now, her generation saw itself as in revolt.

It is possible to speak of the essential conservatism of all poetry, which through its language, its metric, etc., preserves and extends the values of tradition. Yes, but it does so through a paradox: for revolutionary activity is a firm part of that tradition. Catullus, for example, was conservative in that he adopted genres and meters from the past, but to his contemporaries he was revolutionary, for those genres and meters were un-Roman, many of them came from Sappho (the comic Lesbian of lost early Roman plays and hardly the most proper of models), and his subjects ranged from the religiously orthodox to the scandalously personal, with a marked emphasis on the latter.

I want, then, to insist on the obvious, because the obvious is in danger of being forgotten, that what we now call the modernists started by being revolutionary. I want to take a look at the first books of three members of the avant-garde in the years around 1920, H.D.'s *Sea Garden* (1916), Marianne Moore's *Observations* (1924), and Mina Loy's *Lunar Baedecker*[2] (1923). I want especially to isolate these books from the respectability a "collected works" has granted even to Mina Loy by 1988, in an effort to read them as they were when they first appeared. It is of course no chance that the poets I have chosen are women: I am interested also in finding out how women responded in their poetry to being, for probably the first time in history, the comrades and equals of men in a generation of literary innovators.[3]

2

Many of the poems in *Sea Garden* may be called Imagist, but few are as subtle and none are as succinct as the two classic Imagist poems H.D. deliberately omitted, presumably because they did not fit thematically—"Oread" and "The Pool." The book opens with "Sea Rose," one of a series of sea-flower poems, and though it is unquestionably Imagist it is very simply so. To compare it with Rossetti's "The Woodspurge," for instance, shows how straightforward it is. Rossetti's weed serves, for all the mathematical brevity of presentation, as indeed "an intellectual and emotional complex [presented] in an instant of time." Because of a mere habit of observation retained during a period of grief, his plant becomes inextricably associated in his mind with that grief, loaded with an emotion which is irrelevant to the characteristics of the woodspurge itself. By contrast, H.D.'s sea rose, described in an appropriately economical free-verse line, short, qualifying, and nervous, is somewhat allegorical: clearly its enduring and unpretty hardness represents the kind of existence that the poet aspires to.

By sea rose I think she means not a marine plant, real or imagined, but an ordinary rose that has grown too close to the sea to achieve more than a minimal life, contrasted with the "spice rose" inland. She thus announces the sets of opposed images around which most of the book is organized. She is preoccupied with that edge between land and sea embodied in the paradox of the sea garden, where "sea-grass tangles with shore-grass," or where, as she says beautifully, addressing the sea,

> O privet-white, you will paint
> the lintel of wet sand with froth.

They tangle, they interpenetrate, and yet they are irreconcilable. The sea, being in constant movement, is like the bare demands of emotion or of impulse, and is by extension the place of adventure. The land is of course everything else: in "The Helmsman" she refers to "a slender path strung field to field"; land contains the connected, the habitual, even the rational, as opposed to the impulsive. Though at times she speaks with the exasperated folly of a Gothic heroine, in most of the poems she more calmly values the edge between land and sea, because it is the only place at which she apprehends life as not annihilated by too much violence on the one hand or paralyzed by too much security on the other. The symbolism is familiar, but has a certain individuality from her passionate interest in the precarious existence of life-at-the-edge: her sea garden is composed of a number of flowers, real or mythical, whose very names are contradictions—sea rose, sea violet, sea poppy, monsters of endurance. The sea lily is as if carved out of stone by wind-blown sand:

> Sand cuts your petal,
> furrows it with hard edge.

It is an edge at the edge, quintessence of hardness. What she rejects, then, is ease, unstrenuous beauty—the spice rose, the soft grass of the uplands and lowlands, the garden pinks. She rejects honey but approves of the offerings to Priapus which are, as in her Greek source, nuts, shrunken figs, broken pomegranates, crushed grapes, quinces.[4] Such things are also sweet, but theirs is a weathered, aged, abused, distilled, hardened, *enduring* sweetness, one that accords better with the saltiness of the sea.

The soft against the hard, ease against endurance, land against sea, the honeyed sweetness of fresh fruit against the subtler sweetness of nuts or dried fruit; but the book's dualism is not so rigid as I may make it sound. There are inconsistencies, one of them being in the presence, early in the collection, of the unsettling poem "Mid-Day."

"Mid-Day" is both an Imagist poem and a poem about the Imagist procedure, which may be said to consist of extracting images from their context and then treating them in isolation.[5] The speaker is distraught, "anguished—defeated," at the very beginning of the poem. The reader is not told what causes her feeling and suspects that she does not know herself. She experiences a sense of dislocation: identifying first her "thoughts" and then herself with some black "hot shrivelled seeds" ejected from their pods to the paved path. Surely akin to the figs and the rocks, resistant and enduring, they are grouped in this poem with other images of dryness, but here of plants in the dryness of near-annihilation. She contrasts these seeds with a distant poplar, "bright on the hill," burgeoning triumphantly, which in *its* turn is performing a different function from the usual inland plants of *Sea Garden,* being strong and desirable in its fertility. The poem *is* anguished, obsessive, trapped within repetitive perceptions conveyed in repetitive language, and at the same time written with all the energy, tautness, and clarity of the best poems in the collection, the verse movement seeming like that of the speaker's desperate mind. When she gives up at the end, she is indeed defeated:

> O poplar, you are great
> among the hill-stones,
> while I perish on the path
> among the crevices of the rocks.

I have called the poem unsettling, and I do so not only because of its nightmare feeling of helplessness, but also because it implicitly denies all that I know of seeds. They are repositories of life, not the denial of it; the poplar started from a seed, after all; and I have often seen seeds sprouting from the crevices sunken between pavings, a possibility she does not envisage. The sense of the images is inconsistent with the scheme inaugurated by the first poem of the book, according to which you would expect such hard, dry, shriveled things as seeds to possess a more enduring vitality than the soft inland life of the poplar. The anguish of the poem is all too convincing, then, because it seems involuntary.

"Mid-Day" makes the overall plan of imagery in the book

seem *willed*. The tone of most of *Sea Garden* is one, in fact, of a yearning toward the willed images. I want! I want! she cries. I want to be hard because I feel so soft. She admires the rigidity of stone and of statuary. The hero of "The Contest" is seen in terms of chiseled rock, of brass, cypress, white ash. The hero as statue is "Greek," and Greece is a highly symbolic place for H.D.—remote, hard, cool, "perfect." She has no wish to bring ancient Greece up to date, like Joyce; still less to make its terms those of an argument about living values, like Marianne Moore in "An Octopus." Fragments of plot in the less successful poems involve battle, imprisonment, religious ritual, all of a sort far from the experience of her London life. Her Greece (fifth century B.C. as seen by the Victorians) consisted of columns, white drapery, and colorless statuary.

Yet the tone of her yearning is more energetic than the state yearned after. She is typically caught in a state of dismayed wonder at her own helplessness, beseeching powers stronger than herself: "O wind, rend open the heat." She is only a step from whining. A sense of humor would have helped, but that apparently was not available. She keeps things dignified, however, by reverting time after time to the rhythms of incantation. The tone is far from flexible, but is nevertheless impressive, based in a discipline of taut emotion which is in turn measured by an exquisite sense of pace.

What I hope to will into being is not yet here: in a way it is a dream. But in my hope I have already succeeded in distancing myself from the actual, so that it too has become a dream. The imagery of the poems in *Sea Garden* may be simultaneously exact and dreamlike—the black seeds of "Mid-Day," the detached leaf sinking like "a green stone" in "Storm," or the fruit so strangely hindered in "Garden":

> Fruit cannot drop
> through this thick air—
> fruit cannot fall into heat
> that presses up and blunts
> the points of pears
> and rounds the grapes.

She attributes her own claustrophobia to the fruit: the heat is so "thick" that it actually distorts the fruit's original freedom to be what shape it chooses. There is a suggestion of fairy-tale or myth here: Kipling would have called it "How the Pear Lost Its Point." And yet in our world pears *are* blunted, grapes *are* round.—But just a minute, I thought she wanted less malleability, not more? Or is she just unsure of what she wants, sure only that she wants something out of reach? The anxiety which is undercurrent to H.D.'s constant beseeching indicates a terror of the world she lives in, where shape is already determined, however soft the thing taking shape, and where she has little chance of entering the shape and texture of marble in a putative Greece.

As late as 1953 the editors of a British anthology of new poetry considered "Naked Sensitives" a just description of some of its female contributors. That is the way people still expected woman poets to be. And though what was avant-garde in *Sea Garden* was the technical in quite a narrow sense, and though H.D. certainly disturbed no tradition of female *feeling*, yet to see her merely as a naked sensitive, woman as a passive yearner, does not do justice to the individuality of her book. For in an odd way the poetry yearning after what is hard and self-contained, after what does not need to yearn, realizes something of its desire in the very style of its yearning, which is hard it seems with the hardness of desperation and unfulfilled desire.

3

Marianne Moore's first authorized collection, *Observations*, was not published until 1924, and by then she had for several years identified herself with the avant-garde. H.D. was one of the most avant of that garde, and of course she was among Moore's greatest admirers, yet it takes an effort even to consider the two poets in the same sentence. Where *Sea Garden* is anguished, *Observations* is self-possessed. Moore's strong desire for social decorum, for an unprivate speech, paradoxically makes her book far more adventurous than H.D.'s eight years before: in tone, subject matter, metric, and structure of the individual poem, she experiments confidently and widely.

She was considered a difficult poet from the start, as H.D. could hardly have been: and her first unorthodoxy, in the metric, is visible from a mere glance at the pages of the book. Everybody in that experimental generation had individually to make up a free verse of their own. There is no possibility of mistaking the measure of any one of my three woman poets for that of the others. Each has evolved in a distinct fashion. Moore's free verse seems to be influenced by prose writers, her long sentences like those of Henry James receptive to a quantity of physical detail and abstract qualification. When you think of Moore's metric, though, you think primarily of syllabics, which both preceded and succeeded a few years of free verse. The two measures as used by her sound exactly alike (in fact some of her poems that first appeared in the one form were later rewritten in the other), though they looked different on the page, where her syllabics were remarkable for the most shockingly casual enjambments yet to be seen in poetry.

However, "a thing must have intensity." The sentences look loose and wandering, the rhythms look random, but they introduce a whole new type of conversational compactness into poetry. If they are influenced by James, it is by the *spoken* rhythms of the last novels, all of which, I remember, were dictated.

The attitude of the younger Marianne Moore was patrician, in a sense, in that it was half willful and half genuinely eccentric. She waived the whole question of distinctions between verse and prose by treating it as simply irrelevant, and her doing so must have been deeply annoying to those who had always considered that poetry, in its rhythms, diction, and subject matter, should be in some way "elevated." She was obscure, sophisticated, learned, allusive; she wrote to please herself, her mother and brother, and her fellow experimenters; and she emphasized intelligence more than feeling (though there *is* feeling in the poetry, usually just below the surface, and, as Helen Vendler has pointed out in her excellent essay, much of it is painful): you find in Moore, often quite nakedly and separably, what you can only call thought.

It *is* thought too, in the old-fashioned sense, as opposed to the "thoughts" of "Mid-Day," which were not properly anything but fleeting notions, panicked reactions to an unexplained anguish. Yet Moore's thought is often not easy to follow: abstract, subtle, heavily qualified as it is, she may not so much change the subject in the course of a poem as minutely shift the ground of emphasis—stepping very slightly to the side of the subject to address a similar but far from identical matter, as for example at the end of the cat's speech in "My Apish Cousins" (later renamed "The Monkeys").

This last poem brings up the matter of her experiments in poetic structure, which were extraordinarily bold: a few specimens of them may be found in the talking-animal poems in *Observations*, though these are merely specimens, and you might well say that in Moore's poetry there are almost as many structures as there are different poems. "My Apish Cousins" starts with descriptions of animals in a zoo, to pause finally on a cat of vivid presence, who then takes over the second half of the poem with an increasingly complicated speech about art. The style of the poem is one of extreme sophistication; the structure of extreme crudity. That is one of the jokes, of course. The further incongruity, of the speaker with his speech, is another joke, a very broad one. Yet there is no likelihood of its being taken simply as a nonsense poem: the cat is somewhere between the talking animals in Lewis Carroll and those in Dante for, at the same time as she is making her preposterous jokes, Moore seems completely serious in what she gives him to say, however ambiguous it becomes toward the close.

Two other poems in the collection consist of monologues by animals, "Dock Rats" and "Black Earth" (later "Melancthon"), and continue the same combination of joke with serious intent. The first expresses a passion for place through the urbane voice of a rat; the second is a lengthy meditation by an elephant who celebrates the joy of the body, questioning the relation between inner and outer values in a tone both agile and thoughtful. Both poems are exquisitely written and neither has survived into the current "complete" collection of Moore's poems. A fourth poem, "An Octopus," containing a talking jay, has survived, but minus the jay, who acted as an essential though arbitrary link in the original version. There the jay shares a ledge of the mountain with the wild orchid Calypso; the orchid's name is Greek; but the jay "knows no Greek," and therefore cannot converse with her: it is in this way that the reader is introduced to the matter of Greek ethics and style that are taken up in the second half of this long poem. The jay is an associationistic link (a comic one) in an associationistically organized poem. (In the later version there is no link at all but a gap. The reader is left with a juxtaposition of elements that may recall the juxtapositions in Pound's *Cantos*.) This unrevised version is one of the wildest experiments Moore was ever to make in the putting together of a poem: one detail leads to another by, it seems, mere whim, but you are eager to stay with the poem and worry out the meanings because of its sheer attractiveness, line after line.

From about 1917, Moore was thus one of the chief innovators—and possibly, as R. P. Blackmur suggests, taught Pound by her example even as she learned from him. Her most complicated experiment with poetic structure was in one of the latest poems in the book, "Marriage." This is the only place here, moreover, where you might expect Moore to be speaking as a woman. It is possible to imagine finding "female" characteristics elsewhere in her writing, but they are largely asexual, being also present in the writing of a male like Henry James. There are indeed some sharp satirical references to the ways in which men patronize women, notably in "Sojourn in the Whale," where the oppressed stepdaughter is both Ireland and the female sex. But her tone is pretty impersonal, and in that poem there is no use of the first person (though, typically, the second is used several times). When she does say "I" in her poetry, it is not like the "I" of H.D. or Mina Loy, being much closer to the representative first person of the nineteenth-century English essayist. In "Marriage," I have said, you expect Moore to speak as a woman. But she doesn't, exactly, she preserves an apparent distance. In her old age she went so far as to add a note of demurral in the *Complete Poems*, disclaiming personal relevance—this is, she says, simply an accumulation of "statements that took my fancy." Such a remark fools no one. Nobody writes one of her longest poems without some sort of emotional interest in the subject. Barbara Guest believes that it was composed on the occasion of the Bryher-MacAlmon wedding: it is amusing to imagine Moore thinking "if even these two are marrying, maybe it is time to get my feelings straight on the subject."

Getting feelings straight, however, is not an apt description of the poem. In structure it is perhaps unique. Her title suggests an essay, her later demurral a commonplace book. It has been described as a debate; Vendler speaks of it as a vacillating. William Carlos Williams's piercing phrase for it is "an anthology of transit," since it is necessary, as he says, to move rapidly through the poem in reading it. It is not random in arrangement, though: to my mind, Moore preserves a certain balance between Adam and Eve, the husband and wife, favoring—or disfavoring—them about equally. The technique is complicated by the shifting ironies of tone both in Moore's own voice and in the many voices she quotes as she goes along. Hers recurs again and again to a seeming or real impartiality that is impossible to fathom. Marriage, she says in the first sentence, is a thing

> requiring public promises
> of one's intention
> to fulfill a private obligation.

For all the balance of the epigram, it is merely one of those shallow truths that most of us discover in our teens. But it is one point of view, and she is already off on something else: she, and the reader, are already in transit. By the end of the poem marriage has been seen from almost every point of view, and almost always ironically: as a social struggle, as a contest between egos, as a power game—she mentions

> the spiked hand
> that has an affection for one
> and proves it to the bone.

The one point of view not taken explicitly into account, as Blackmur noted fifty years ago, is the sexual, which is referred to only through the conventional emblems of the apple (as in Eden) and the fire (as in St. Paul). The poem ends with the image of a successful marriage, only possible as the result of the statesmanship of "an archaic Daniel Webster," under whose statue is written

> "Liberty and union
>   now and forever";
>
> the Book on the writing-table;
> the hand in the breast-pocket.

One must be of positively archaic simplicity to be able to accept it, she suggests. The flexible and subtle emulator of James is hardly interested in a union as fixed as a crude statue, its terms as permanent and frozen as the stone Bible before it and the immovable half-concealed hand of the male whose mind is made up—values absolute, unchangeable, taken for granted.

I am not trying to suggest that Moore was a moral relativist—she was anything but, yet she makes it clear in another poem how much she valued "accessibility to experience." To resist marriage, to remain flexible, she had to be even harder than the statue of Daniel Webster, hard as the armored animals that flocked into her poetry as she got older, protecting herself from the surrounding pressures: she would not marry; she would not give up her options. Neither would she, when she could help it, write as a woman any more than as a man; and so one of her forms of courage in *Observations* is to write virtually without gender. There is nothing wrong with that; after all, it is what many men do all the time. She is merely claiming as her own one of the privileges of the male.

4

In "O Hell" Mina Loy rejects the "excrements" of the past with a stylish defiance. The careful condensation of her lan-

uage qualifies what might appear to us a childish iconoclasm.
o us, perhaps, but hardly to the reader of the 1920s: for even
he steadiest among that generation seem to have felt unbear-
bly hampered by the sheer weight of the Victorian inheri-
ance, and showed an almost hysterical impatience to throw it
ut into the street.

Yet it is not as "modern" a poem as it looks. I would sug-
est, first, that the title is not a flapper's expletive, but rather a
memory of (or reference to) that Blakean hell which is the
ome of energy as opposed to the establishment church of
eaven. After all, in another poem the poet sees herself as
ostracized . . . with God."[6] And there are other echoes from
he Marriage of Heaven and Hell: in line 6, "Our person is a
overed entrance to infinity," and in the last sentence the linea-
nents of desire become divine: she evokes "Goddesses and
oung Gods" (provocatively placing the female before the
nale!).

No writer passively inherits "the" tradition, you make your
wn choices, your own incongruous combinations of literary
arents. If in this poem Loy takes Blake as iconoclastic spon-
or for her iconoclasm, she elsewhere claims relationship to
nore recent poets like Laforgue. It is the present she empha-
izes, aligning herself deliberately and almost programmati-
ally with the avant-garde by including in *Lunar Baedecker* a
roup of poems praising Joyce, Brancusi, and Wyndham
ewis.

Her contemporaries often compared her with Marianne
Moore—naturally enough, since they were both clever women
vho had started publishing at about the same time. Each had
leveloped her own inimitable kind of free verse, neither went
in fear of abstractions," both tended toward the epigram-
natic. Yet, for all the resemblances, what a difference!

The poem "Lunar Baedeker," a witty guide to the moon
s literary symbol, consists of a series of details that are simul-
aneously both image and epigram. It is an effect special to
oy, to be perfected in her poem of World War II, "Omen of
Victory." The rather jerky emphases of the short verses suit
he overall tone of self-conscious cleverness. Frequency of
djectives, alliteration, internal rhyme and half-rhyme, a dan-

dyish fondness for the obscure epithet—all contribute to a tone of deliberate artificiality. The clotted phrases do not seek to look unstudied, and could never occur in the midst of Moore's equally elaborate discourse, with *its* air of conversational improvisation.

The greatest difference is to be found in her attitude toward the human body. For H.D. it was sublimated into emblems like the sea rose; for Moore it did not exist; for Loy it was a necessary part of her subject matter. Not that she thought of sexuality as just a matter of mutual fondlings in the sunshine; she and "Johannes" in "Love Songs" are far from the divine adolescents of "O Hell."

The full thirty-four part sequence of "Love Songs" that had been printed in the magazine *Others* in 1917 was greatly abridged in the book versions published during Loy's life, but I agree with Virginia M. Kouidis (in *Mina Loy, American Modernist Poet*) that the long version is preferable and, moreover, should be read as a single poem, repetitive disillusionment its rhythm and subject. All forms of it, in any case, open with the lines:

> Spawn of Fantasies
> Sifting the appraisable
> Pig Cupid
> His rosy snout
> Rooting erotic garbage

The reader's initial disorientation resulting from Loy's lack of punctuation is an essential part of the meaning. It is appropriate to the shifting and indecisive nature of romantic love. Does "sifting" belong to Cupid, purposeful with his phallic snout, or to the fantasies, daydreams reviewing themselves like pornographic tapes? Both are possibilities, and, in keeping them open, Loy looks forward, as she does in other ways, to later developments of experimental poetry. The work shifts constantly between possibilities, specifically between those of fantasy and reality, and Kouidis suggests that it thus shows considerable resemblance to "Prufrock" (though dates preclude the likelihood of influence one way or the other). There is this difference, however: Prufrock's are merely speculative fantasies, but the speaker of "Love Songs" has a real love affair. The longer version of the poem ends with the line "Love—the preeminent littérateur": whether as Pig or literary hack, Cupid will always be making busy work for himself. Thus, while Prufrock will return to his speculative fantasy, the speaker of "Love Songs" will return to her attempts to substantiate her fantasy. They are both idealists, but she deals with actual events and is, moreover, energetic in speech to the very end.

Loy writes as a woman, and as a woman standing up for herself. She does not do so as dutiful follower of a political program, but as expression of a quite unforced indignation at the comedy of male complacency, and not incidentally as exploration of new poetic material, of which the potential excites her as a writer. The battle of the sexes in "Love Songs" is between "shuttle-cock and battle-door," a phrase compact with contemporary daring and undated wit. In "Parturition," which would count among her best work if it were cut by half, she writes what I take to be the first poem ever about experiencing labor pains and childbirth. And in "Sketch of a Man on a Platform" she satirizes with admirable vigor the man who is busy, *too* busy, at being a man.

For all her aggressive modernism and feminism, she identifies with a traditional genre more easily than most of her great contemporaries—that of satire. Her satire is never so absolute as in "Der Blinde Junge," which I readily follow Yvor Winters and Kenneth Fields in considering her most moving achievement.

It may be conveniently set against another poem in the collection, "Ignoramus," an attractive combination of languages recalling nursery rhyme, philosophy, polite small talk, and Rimbaud-like dream excursion. Its subject, an idealized tramp, the Clown of Fortune, owes something perhaps to the Shakespearean fool, his idiom the cunning wisdom of the innocent. "Breakfasting on rain," he is a cheerful vagabond who has created a satisfactory alternative world of his own. There is no hint of idealization, however, in "Der Blinde Junge," which is about another of the vagrants that fascinated

Loy all her life, a blind beggar on a Vienna sidewalk after World War I. The poem is written with a relentless bitterness. The Futurist conception of war as a global hygiene, with which Loy had possibly flirted some years before, is dismissed at the start of the poem, thirteen words punctuated with a blunt rhythm that is almost no rhythm and merely emphasizing, it seems, the uncompromising nature of the statement made:

> The dam Bellona
> littered
> her eyeless offspring
> Kriegsopfer
> upon the pavements of Vienna

War is no goddess working toward either hygiene or glory, but a slovenly animal that "litters" the street with her "litter," human puppies born blind and staying blind, whom it immediately abandons, offerings like this youth,

> this slow blind face
> pushing its virginal nonentity
> against the light

The dim questing movement is scarcely human. The phrase "virginal nonentity" combines powerfully with the specifics to sharpen the accuracy of the observation: he is merely a virgin to the complex life allowed the entities passing by. In the lines,

> Pure purposeless eremite
> of centripetal sentience,

it might seem for a moment, even, that her contempt has turned against the pathetic youth himself, but it has not, being still directed against the forces that made him pathetic. She uses arcane vocabulary to deadly effect. "Eremite" suggests the Keats of "Bright Star," but she uses it with a difference: for the self-containment of the hermit, like that of the virgin, has been brought about not by a choice but by a maiming. Implicitly she attacks the values of a culture through such words, embedded as they are in the classics of our poetry. The lines that follow look at first glance even more impersonal—perhaps affectedly so—but reading them aloud you realize that the greater sweep of their rhythm suggests the growing scope of her indignation: in them she describes, by showing its termination, the delicate mechanism of the sighted human being. "Horologe" and "index" indicate that it *is* a mechanism, but "carnose" and "tendon" that it is an organic one, too sensitive for repair:

> Upon the carnose horologe of the ego
> the vibrant tendon index moves not
>
> since the black lightning desecrated
> the retinal altar

If you are used to the immediate effects of an Ann Sexton, then of course such writing cannot stay you. But if you take the poem as slowly as one by H.D. or Moore, you see that such language cannot be improved on for that kind of compression that is the peculiar property of poetry. The sensitive mechanism has its holiness, she goes on to say—and the connection of holiness with the *wholeness* of the adolescent body is already familiar from "O Hell." This adolescent, however, is no young god, but a dreadful abandoned puppy.

> A downy youth's snout
> nozzling the sun
> drowned in dumfounded instinct

She ends the poem with what starts as a conventional didactic address, but its iambic eloquence is interrupted by the deliberate lameness of the last line, recalling her from the temple of rhetoric to the mere fact on the sidewalk:

> Listen!
> illuminati of the colored earth
> how this expressionless "thing"
> blows out damnation and concussive dark
>
> Upon a mouth organ

There is a brilliant etymological pun on "illuminati"; and another pun on "blow out," for the youth tries to *extinguish* the great terrors by *blowing out* through the apertures of his mouth organ (or harmonica), producing the least eloquent of music, something like the whine of the baby animal. Which brings you back to the beginning again.

Pity may be evoked by the poem, and it inevitably is, but it isn't *in* it. Loy is a tough writer, and sentiment in the usual sense is seldom present in her work. Her overt feeling in this poem is of contempt, turned upon the rest of us, the illuminati reading her poem, complacently assuming that we are heirs to all culture. She has come far from simple iconoclasm, and equally far from the Laforguian self-cancellations of "Love Songs": she is hard, pure, unrelenting. The controlled anger and indignation of the poem make it the equal, to my mind, of the best of Pope or Swift.[7]

5

Hardness was a quality sought after by the avant-garde poet during the period marked approximately by the years 1910 to 1925. It was considered a corrective to what appeared the softness of the poetry in the years preceding. It took the form of an emphasis on clarity, explicitness, and sharpness of language and image, accompanied by an equal emphasis on objectivity or the appearance of it: at that time Pound, Williams, and Eliot were much taken with analogies between science and poetry.

That is a summary of what everybody knows already. My impression, however, is that women, aware of certain stereotypes about female passivity, felt understandably even more compromised than the men by the real and imagined softness of writing before 1910. It is perhaps relevant to recall here that in the anthology which Pound assembled late in life, *Confucius to Cummings,* his one woman poet from the nineteenth century was Mrs. Browning rather than Emily Dickinson or even Christina Rossetti. No wonder his female contemporaries needed to show that they could write hard poetry too.

"We were not conforming to anything," Marianne Moore recalled; and so in reaction—who is to say how far conscious?—these three women published their astonishing early poetry: H.D.'s representing the hardness of passivity, Marianne Moore's the hardness of resistance, and Mina Loy's the hardness of aggression. Later, in different ways, their poetry softened somewhat, and none of them, in my view, often approached again the concentrated brilliance of their first work.

Nevertheless, in that work they established, I hope for good, that hardness is not the prerogative of male poetry. As various writers have pointed out, hardness, softness, and derivative terms used in literary criticism look back to an obviously sexual origin. But there is no reason that good woman poets should be limited by the symbols of gender. If Jane Austen hadn't been in the novel, then they needn't be in poetry, another state in what is, after all, a free country.

NOTES

1. Interview with Donald Hall, *A Marianne Moore Reader* (New York: Viking, 1961), p. 266.

2. This was the spelling of the book's title.

3. I refer to "woman poets" throughout. Three male poets I admire, Basil Bunting, Donald Davie, and August Kleinzahler, have tried to retain or revive the word poetess, but I find it impossible to use here, since it is not without its associations, and they are precisely those that Moore and Loy were trying to escape from.

4. Joan Retallack, in "H.D., H.D.," *Parnassus* 12, no. 2 and 13, no. 1 (1985), pp. 70–71, compares the passage in H.D.'s poem with its Greek source.

5. I echo Kenneth Fields in this sentence, Introduction to H.D.'s *Tribute to Freud* (Boston: Godine, 1974), p. xxix.

6. I perhaps wrongly interpret "with" as "by." Mina Loy's use of prepositions is unusual elsewhere as well.

7. There is one collection of Mina Loy's poetry in print, *The Last Lunar Baedeker,* published by the Jargon Society in 1982 and Carcanet Press in 1985, edited by Roger Conover. For its existence I cannot be too grateful, all the more because Conover has made substantial additions of poems never before available in book form; but it can hardly be said to contain a critical text, and there are many typographical errors. These errors are the more serious in that the

reader has little opportunity to compare this text with any other; so I append a list of the more serious below, supplying emendations either from other printed versions or from my own guesses.

Conover edition, p.3, 10: *to* should read *of* (as in Kouidis)
p. 8, 8: *is* should be *in*
p.21, 1: *satinize* should be *satirize*
p.57, 1: *Peninsular* should be *Peninsula* (?)
p.63, 18: *magneta* should be *magenta*
p.91, 2: *sitting* should be *sifting* (but Kouidis has *silting*)
p.180, 18: *interstate* should be *intestate* (?)
p.182, 7: *efflugence* should be *effulgence*

What the Slowworm Said
Eliot, Pound, and Bunting

1

This century more than any other has been fascinated by "the primitive." Its artists have been especially drawn to the idea of a ceremony, or a sequence of ceremonies, which sums up at the same time birth, sexuality, procreation, and death. Their fascination has led some into violent fictions, where the emphasis has been less on birth and procreation than on sexuality and death. An example is D. H. Lawrence's story "The Woman Who Rode Away." The Woman, the wife of an industrialist in Mexico, stunned to a boredom transcending boredom by her comfortable but meaningless and confined existence, rides off to a distant mythical valley where "the old priests still kept up the ancient religion," with the object of offering herself up as a ritual sacrifice, though she may not be explicitly aware of her own intention until she is already in the hands of the Indians. Once she is made captive she comes in contact with men only. The feeling of the story is erotic although the action is not. In the ceremonies that lead up to her sacrifice (here she is receiving a ritual massage), "She knew she was a victim; that all this elaborate work upon her was the work of victimising her. But she did not mind. She wanted it." As elsewhere in the best of Lawrence's fiction, the improbable story is kept insistently alive by his imaginative fidelity to

Reprinted from *The Occasions of Poetry,* expanded edition (San Francisco: North Point Press, 1985), and from *PN Review* 27 (1982).

53

states of mind, however unusual, and by his feeling for the startling visual image. In front of the cave where the final sacrifice is to be performed hangs an enormous "dripping, fang-like spoke of ice." The identification of the anthropomorphic *fang* with the metallic *spoke* is wonderful. From within the cave the priest watches "in absolute motionlessness . . . till the red sun should send his ray through the column of ice." Its doing so will be the signal for her death.

It was the mark of Lawrence's boldness that he was prepared to follow through what he had started, so that he can show us without flinching how a more heightened life might be found in the preparation for a death that is in some way significant. The implication is thus that the heightened life and the death are in some way the same thing. It was Lawrence's limitation that such an equivalence is practically meaningless, certainly in the terms he gives.

The trouble with his story is that he is trying to believe in a myth which he has made up by an act of will. He doesn't really believe in it, and nor do we: we all know that the woman's death is not going to give the Indians power over the white race, and he knows it too. The fictional characters believe it, but that makes them merely pathetic. Such pathos is scarcely recognized, if at all, in the story, which is taken up rather by descriptions of the Indians' grandeur, of the preparations for the sacrifice, and of the woman's interesting state of mind. The real connection of the story with common experience is not through any sense we may have of regeneration or self-renewal but through our secret desires for self-destruction.

One way of looking at the story is as a kind of extreme variation on the century's concern with real or fantasized vegetation ceremony and fertility rite. That concern has become such a commonplace that the very phrases I have just used smack of the English class. A few years ago a teacher friend gave an amusing account of a literary conference where speaker after speaker talked about symbols of fertility, speaker after speaker looking tired, desiccated, and in person completely beyond the task of promulgating such fertility. Yet the emphasis of the good critics was appropriate enough: just as when an individual growing beyond his own youth may thereupon start to be attracted by the young, as possessing some-thing he no longer possesses, so when we have made the social divorce from our origins most final, our imaginations start to dwell compulsively on primitive society and whatever we think its ways may have been. We may recall that Picasso's interest in African masks, Stravinsky's ballet music *Le Sacre du Printemps,* and Eliot's *Waste Land* all come within ten years.

Nor has our interest flagged. The pattern of interdepen-dence between fertility and death still has plenty of meaning for us. In *Briggflatts* (1965), Basil Bunting says

> Decay thrusts the blade,
> wheat stands in excrement
> trembling.

I find more complexity in these two and a half lines than in the whole of Lawrence's story. It is a paradox that decay, strong in its very disintegration, can perform an action as energetic as *thrust.* Conversely, though the wheat stands stur-dily in excrement, it does so *trembling,* tentative in its very vigor. And a few years before *Briggflatts,* Robert Duncan, in "Nor is the Past Pure" (*The Opening of the Field,* 1960), calls Kore, goddess of regeneration, the "Queen of the Midden-heap," and goes on to say that "Death is prerequisite to the birth of grass." My point is that though both Bunting's and Duncan's statements are exact and accurate, perhaps even obvious, they are not lines that any poet would have been likely to write in the eighteenth or nineteenth centuries. They emerge directly out of a twentieth-century preoccupation.[1]

2

As at one time poets spoke of the Matter of Britain or the Matter of France, referring to bodies of subject matter consid-ered suitable for romance or epic, so we might speak of the Matter of Fertility, which was for some time—perhaps still is—a central portion of the Modernist legacy. It was estab-lished as such by the reputation of *The Waste Land,* which swiftly became so famous, so representative of the new poetry, that for many years it partially eclipsed from view the achievements of several of Eliot's contemporaries. *The Waste Land* was Modern Poetry, not only for the philistine in the street, but also for the poets. William Carlos Williams had dreamed of another kind of Modernism, and he was angry not only that Eliot had taken the direction he had, but that *The Waste Land* was so good that one couldn't possibly disregard it. And it was to the nostalgia of *The Waste Land* that Hart Crane was addressing himself with the heroic optimism of *The Bridge*.

As Eliot tells us, the structure of his poem is based loosely on Jessie Weston's account of the Grail stories as disguised vegetation ceremonies, but if the poem deals with the primitive, it does so from the point of view of one who has grown too far beyond it ever to go back to it. Eliot cannot go back to it, even in imagination. At the same time, worldly, nervous, complicatedly ironic, he sees the present as fatally diminished—and doing that is the same as seeing a diminishing of possibility itself. But one must not discount an extraordinary sonority in the writing, a Jacobean-Symbolist rhetoric in which the old stage props of rats and skulls may be used for simultaneous ironic and dramatic purposes.

Beside *The Waste Land* I would like to consider Pound's Canto 47, written in the early 1930s. No doubt I am doing it a certain violence in extracting it from its place among the rest of the *Cantos*, for it constantly takes up and renews motifs from earlier in the series and introduces motifs to be echoed later. Nevertheless, once the violence is done, it does stand magnificently on its own as an independent poem.

What was the original relation between it and *The Waste Land* in Pound's mind? It is impossible to know. It was Pound, after all, who had cut *The Waste Land* into its present shapely form out of the cumbrous manuscript *He Do the Police in Different Voices* that Eliot had sent him in 1922, and so he had been in a sense a collaborator on the finished work. I find it difficult not to speculate that he is consciously trying to deal once more with much of the same Fraser-and-Weston matter of primitive belief and ceremony, with the death and rebirth of the god, but coming at it from a different direction, coming at it in fact through the related concerns of many of the first forty-six Cantos.

One marked resemblance between the two works is found in the prominent place given by each to the (in every sense) shadowy presence of Tiresias. Pound evokes him in the first line of the Canto, through the voice of Circe: "Who even dead, yet hath his mind entire!" For emphasis he excerpts the line from where it originally occurred in the Homeric speech he is about to translate in the following lines, so as to place it at the head of the Canto. Yet Tiresias remains the vaguest of presences: perhaps he introduces the Canto because he is the container of knowledge, and thus by implication of much of the received wisdom which is about to be quoted from people like Hesiod. In this way he would have something of the same structural purpose as the Tiresias of *The Waste Land*, where Eliot's note reads, "what Tiresias *sees*, in fact, is the substance of the poem." Eliot's Tiresias is presented more physically:

> I Tiresias, old man with wrinkled dugs
> Perceived the scene, and foretold the rest—
> I too awaited the expected guest.
> He, the young man carbuncular, arrives . . .

The presentation produces contrast, and the contrast is ironic—rather vulgarly so, I have always thought, because Eliot's disdain of the ordinary is rooted in the vulgarity of the snob. *The Waste Land* is built on such contrasts and the merging of such contrasts. Tiresias contrasts and merges with the typist who awaits the expected guest; mad Ophelia leaving the throne room contrasts and merges with Lou and May leaving the pub at closing time. The irony pervading the work usually arises from such sources.

Pound also proceeds by juxtapositions. He would hardly be the mature Pound if he didn't. But the juxtapositions are not here for ironic contrast, rather they are different aspects of the same subject, enforcing each other. The subject of the whole Canto, as I have implied, seems to be "ancient knowledge and wisdom": Circe's speech; references to different kinds of festival and ceremony; archaic didactic maxims about the sexes or the sowing of grain; fragmentary addresses to Adonis from lines ascribed to Bion. What they have in common is that all bear on the connection between death and fertility.

The writing is much like this:

> The sea is streaked red with Adonis,
> The lights flicker red in small jars.
> Wheat shoots rise new by the altar,
> flower from the swift seed.

It is the method that was first employed in *Cathay:* a picture (or an exclamation or a statement of fact or of feeling) to a line, and often an independent clause to a line. The image is represented with great economy, rather than being explored sensuously as it was for example in the second Canto, where "god sleight" was shown to us through all the senses. The mind ranges through variety rather than dwelling on the richness of individual perceptions.

The Stone Age wisdom is untouched by the twentieth century until just over half way through, where the writing goes through a change that at first seems small but is actually a turning point in the Canto. It does so during instructions concerning oxen:

> Two oxen are yoked for ploughing
> Or six in the hill field
> White bulk under olives, a score for drawing down stone,
> Here the mules are gabled with slate on the hill road.
> Thus was it in time.

The personal perception has entered, brief but suggestive, and less immediately functional than the perception of the tribe. We were not told what the wheat shoots looked like as they rose by the altar, but we are told about the oxen and the mules. *Bulk* is what Pound has noticed for himself, we can ourselves almost see the thick heavy slow bodies of the oxen pale under the darker trees, and in the next line we come to something Pound surely glimpsed in the Italy where he lived, "Here . . . on the hill road," he sees the mules "gabled with slate" with a sudden individual immediacy. "Thus was it in time," he goes on, implying that as he sees it today, so it has always been.

In this second phase of the poem, then, the prehistoric tribal perception is juxtaposed against the modern personal perception, and the utterance, though not inconsistent with what came before, is weighted with the experience of the senses, having precisely that richness and immediacy that Pound has deliberately kept out of the earlier phase.

We find a speaker standing on a terrace. He stands there as he could have stood at any time in history. The starlike blossoms of the olive trees fall to the ground, suggesting that—as the earth wheels beneath the sky—the stars themselves fall through the branches. The Canto is marked now by a certain sadness that death is part of the natural process. The speaker thinks of the martin *floating*, almost as much in his mind as in his perception.

> His wing-print is black on the roof tiles
> And the print is gone with his cry.

The image reminds me of early surrealist movies, Cocteau's or Buñuel's, almost contemporary with this Canto. The print is here, the print is gone. Now it floats only in memory, memory that is only slightly less transient than the martin.

"Hast thou found a nest softer than cunnus?" In the Jonsonian questions that follow, the utterance is that of a man on his own who has arrived at the complicated awareness of human passion and human transience as each conditional on the other. But in the last part of the Canto, through an ecstasy partly religous and partly orgasmic, the speaker, whether singular or compound, enters the experience of the tribe again, though strengthened now, perhaps, by his understanding. The personal is now combined with the tribal. A composite ceremony is suggested, in which we move from rite to rite, from religion to religion, from country to country, but the gist is the same and the passion is the same. Each image is both sharp in itself and yet inclusive: "By this door have I entered the hill." There is no sense of the fragmentary, but rather of

coherence. Where in *The Waste Land* Eliot is permanently exiled from such ceremonies, Pound both creates them and enters what he has created, with his full imagination, having
gone as it were behind the backs of the anthropologists. The
Canto is a poem about experience where the earlier poem is
about the thwarting of experience. Orgasm is not just for the
young man carbuncular and the typist. "Give, sympathise,
control" are not just abstract exhortations translated from the
wordless thunder, they are—though literally unuttered—
central to the full rich experience of Canto 47.

3

In an interview Basil Bunting says of Pound, "The lights drifting out to sea in the festival of Rapallo he does beautifully; I
was the first to do that but my poem was too bad and I tore it
up."[2] Like most other readers, I had always taken the drifting
lights in Canto 47 to be part of some imagined ancient peasant
ritual, but in a sense this new information about their source
doesn't change my original reading: they still suggest the
same kind of context in the poem that they did in the first
place.

Meanwhile Bunting's work had for some time been haunted
by echoes from Eliot. He does not appear to have particularly
liked Eliot, and he speaks in a review of 1932 about the sneer-
ing tone so common in *The Waste Land,* but he was for a while
more profoundly influenced by the style of that poem than by
anything of his friend and teacher, Pound. *Briggflatts* was not to
come until more than thirty years later, and in so far as it takes
on the Matter of Fertility it does so not only less directly and
consciously than any of the work I have mentioned but also in
an entirely different way. Where Pound, in Canto 47, deals with
the representative—for even the man on the terrace is Pound
only as representative of an individual awareness—Bunting
deals with the specific, the young lovers, the young man as
"poet appointed," Antonietta, Hastor (whom I take to be Lord
Astor of the Cliveden Set), Scarlatti, Eric Bloodaxe. The poem
is so dense with the specific that there is as much danger of

doing it violence by extracting one motif for consideration as there was in taking one Canto out of the collected *Cantos*.

To say that this "autobiography" consists of specifics is not to claim that any of it is necessarily a literal transcription from Bunting's own life. On the contrary—one of the "plaited lines" of its motifs reveals material fully as exotic as a human sacrifice in Mexico, the Chapel Perilous, or the rites of Adonis. In the third section of the poem Alexander the Great climbs the mountain at the end of the earth to find the massive figure of Israfel, the angel of death, "lit feathers sweeping snow," perpetually poised with raised trumpet and swelled cheeks to blow the blast that will bring the end of the world. The legend, it appears, is Islamic, but when Alexander falls stunned from the mountain, Bunting has him fall to a ground very like that of Northumberland. As he lies there, Alexander, the Achiever, hears the song of the slowworm at his ear—and the slowworm sings, among other things, "I prosper / lying low." The song gives Alexander pause:

> So he rose and led home silently through clean woodland
> where every bough repeated the slowworm's song.

It is the song of the natural world, which is clean of the achiever and his ambition, and which is also helpless before him.

Alexander and Bunting's other achievers (like those in *The Spoils*) are the exact opposite to the anonymous Adonis worshippers of Canto 47, among whom we could without much ingenuity number the slowworm and the pubescent lovers in *Brigflatts*. The lovers are "gentle" and "generous."

> Rainwater from the butt
> she fetches and flannel
> to wash him inch by inch,
> kissing the pebbles.
> Shining slowworm part of the marvel.

The activity of the verse itself, like the activity it describes, is deliberate, careful, and pleasurable. The pleasure is not a silky one, however: it is a touch abrasive, as the rough surface of a flannel feels on skin. The short lines have to be read slowly for the sake of clarity—we must pause a moment after the word *fetches*, to prevent it from seeming part of a parallel construction with *flannel;* "to wash him inch by inch" can not be hurried over because of the closeness of the *sh* and *ch* sounds. The pebbles are the boy's balls, the slowworm his cock, "part of the marvel" (for the pure at heart the commonest thing is marvelous). They are associated with the other evidences of "the fells' late spring," with the bull that opens the poem, "ridiculous and lovely" in his dance, with what is unpracticed and uncalculating, with what acts on impulse through a trust that is source both of strength and vulnerability. It is already vulnerable: "wheat stands in excrement / trembling." And it will continue to be, for the boy must necessarily grow up into the achiever who knows the need for guile, into an "adult male of a merciless species."

Thus we are led into the rest of the poem, including the tale of Alexander in the middle, but including much else—a world of matter as compressed as in any poem written in English. The work is complex and dense, yet it is not really difficult to the reader who has the least interest in pursuing the motifs, for the density starts yielding at once to the human voice.

The abstract imperatives of "What the Thunder Said" occur near the end of *The Waste Land,* and they are not in any way "acted on" in that poem: but Bunting tells us what the slowworm said in the middle of *Briggflatts,* giving his protagonist a chance to do something about it. Do what? The slowworm was associated with his own youthful body, but he as an adult identifies himself with the rat, "accustomed to penury, / filth, disgust, and fury." But it is possible to learn: even he can "lie low" for a moment, and—asking "nothing but silence" like the Quaker—can, returned to his original starting point in the North of England, put aside achievement long enough to pay attention through the senses to the natural physical world. And thus it is that the last section of this sonata that is also an autobiography moves into its vision of the continuous fecundity of the earth, in roughly the same geographical area as that in which we encountered the intermingled images of love and death at the outset: consequently the vision includes them too when a little later echoes from them are heard. For Eliot the fecundity was in a past beyond recapture; for Pound it was in a past that could be entered by the imagination which had brought it into being; and for Bunting it is in a past not only recaptured and reentered by the imagination but literally prolonged:

> Shepherds follow the links,
> sweet turf studded with thrift;
> fell-born men of precise instep
> leading demure dogs
> from Tweed and Till and Teviotdale,
> with hair combed back from the muzzle,
> dogs from Redesdale and Coquetdale
> taught by Wilson or Telfer.
> Their teeth are white as birch,
> slow under black fringe
> of silent, accurate lips.
> The ewes are heavy with lamb.
> Snow lies bright on Hedgehope
> and tacky mud about Till
> where the fells have stepped aside
> and the river praises itself,
> silence by silence sits
> and Then is diffused in Now.

It is like an old dream of order, but it is still a fact in the present, that is in the early 1960s in Northumberland: the hierarchy of shepherds over sheepdogs, of sheepdogs over sheep. Every perception, every movement described, has the easy *exactness* of familiar recurrence—the turf *studded* with the herb thrift, men of *precise* instep, dogs with *accurate* lips: in this specific and fecund scene, seeming spontaneity is a reenactment of tradition; each detail recognizes its relation to each other detail, and is at ease in that established relation. Bunting's comparison of the dogs' teeth to the color of birchbark is as much a matter of course as the dogs' relation to their masters and to the sheep. It takes genius to recognize the interrelatedness of the scene but, once it is recognized, in a sense all else is found.

In his last section of *Briggflatts* Bunting is in a position from which he can see the right rhythms as continuing—in the seasons, in the tides, in the scene of the dogs with the pregnant ewes, later in the stars themselves. "Then is diffused in Now." He has recovered those rhythms in the present, and more than Pound has recovered them in terms not only of the imagination but of literal fact. This is the sense in which *Briggflatts* is autobiography: he has arrived at the essential beginnings by returning to his own beginnings. It is not a permanent arrival. The Coda, if nothing else, would take care of such a cheerful notion. But the arrival is possible, and perhaps only in such terms as these.

I am not trying to say that Bunting's poem is better than Eliot's or Pound's. Certainly *The Waste Land* has meant too much to several generations of readers, and Canto 47 means too much to me, that I should want to supplant them. But *Briggflatts* addresses itself to certain of the same barely formulable needs of ours as they do. We seek some kind of reconciliation with our beginnings, or at least an understanding of how such a reconciliation might be brought about; and so the Matter of Fertility came into being, which has sometimes been interpreted so simplistically that it was merely an excuse for devising an erotic human sacrifice. In *Briggflatts* Bunting— among his many other achievements there—shows us a full reconciliation, though brief, tentative, and qualified by its own transience. Ceremony has matured to tradition; the representative man has become the specific man of autobiography; a montage of places has become one place. He does indeed show us.

NOTES

1. The exception among nineteenth-century poets was Whitman, who foreshadowed and influenced Lawrence, Bunting, and Duncan. These poets might superficially seem to repeat an orthodox religious theme, but when George Herbert wrote in "Vertue" that the rose's "root is ever in its grave," he meant something different,

referring to the fact that the Christian's death is the source of his everlasting spiritual life.

2. "Basil Bunting obiter dicta," collected by Dale Reagan, *Basil Bunting: Man and Poet* (Orono, Maine: National Poetry Foundation, 1981), p. 267.

As If Startled Awake

The Poetry of Janet Lewis

1

Reading a poet almost unanthologized, like Janet Lewis, you find you have an enviable freedom. You can stray from garden to garden of her *Poems Old and New* and the subsequent *Late Offerings,* admiring the contents without being halted by recognitions, as of anthology poem here, teachable poem there. That there are "major" poems in these collections, as major as you might ask for, I have no doubt at all, but you will have to identify them for yourself. Meanwhile you read on without preconceptions, enjoying at large with an open judgment, and appreciating the way major and minor grow together in mutual dependence.

An early poem, "The Tennis Players," catches the eye. It is masterly, the way the movement of the players is conveyed by the movement of the verse, which leads you irresistibly into the activity of her memory. This is its beginning:

> Their flying feet are swift
> And silent, and the lift
> Of shoulder and of arm
> And body without weight;
> And radiant with charm
> They play beyond the gate
> Upon the shadowed lawn.

Reprinted from *Numbers* 6–7 (Winter 1988–90).

The irregular energy of the players is not contained precisely inside the lines, but spills over endings. Each of these endings does find its rhyme, but in a pattern less predictable than that of, for example, a dance. The poem therefore has an internal restlessness, however neat and enclosed it looks on the page. And for all the precision of language a slight instability is caused by the word "charm," which in effect asserts but limits the players' claim on her attention. I think I find a similar effect, of uncertain qualification, in the word "dreaming," which opens the penultimate line:

> Dreaming I watch them yet
> Across a continent.

The at best half-rhyme of the final word and the consequent partial loss of harmony suggest an awareness that what is woken from at this point is only a daydream, a reverie of ideal grace more perfect than its original.

This poem, like many others by Lewis, reminds me of a passage in one of her novels, *The Trial of Sören Qvist,* where Anna, the protagonist's daughter, is walking home in the early evening before May Day:

> She walked with a wonderful lightness and awareness in all her body, as if her blood ran quicker, her hearing were more acute, her eyes more swift and clear than usual. It was as if she had been startled awake, as, after moments of sudden and temporary fear, or of brief anger, the body seems to have leaped into a quickened state of being. But she, strangely enough, had passed from a moment of shame into a state of exquisite vitality.

The body's generous consciousness of itself is at the heart of both Lewis's poetry and her fiction, and is responsible for the somewhat Tolstoyan feel you sometimes get in her novels. The body's pleasure is defined by awareness of its own bounds, in which it rejoices, since those bounds are precisely what enable it to participate with such fullness in the outer world. Through its doors of perception, cleansed, everything appears as it is, finite. Moreover, the pleasure is given its very edge by contrast—in this case contrast with the feelings it succeeds. Many of her poems start from the body in this way, even in her ninth decade drawing from "a quickened sense of being" and an "exquisite vitality" of perception.

My guess is that in "The Tennis Players," Lewis is remembering a scene from the Michigan of her youth while writing in the entirely different landscape of Santa Fe in the early 1920s. Because of the acuteness of her physical sympathies, which enter the very verse movement, her nostalgia is a vigorous one, containing within its own vigor the germ of a critique against itself. She recalls a certain lawn, "beyond the gate," in one of the lost gardens of childhood; and from beginning to end, Lewis's poetry is full of small yards planted with flowers and herbs, often edging meadows and orchards. The hot summers of those gardens conduce to dream, but dream, oddly, in which the intelligence roams at will, by no means put to sleep.

2

You can bask in your nostalgia, so that it becomes an end in itself. Lewis does not do so, for, if it is caused by separation, she is concerned wherever possible to link things up again. That is why I called it, even in that early poem, a vigorous nostalgia. And if she dreams in gardens crowded with the "gaudy flowers" of Europe, she is also aware that they were the dwelling places of American Indians only a generation or two before. Quite as much as the anonymous authors of the medieval carols she admires so much, they are precursors— but precursors who have been displaced, and she is intent throughout her career in establishing our connections with them.

Her first short collection (1922) was in fact called *Indians in the Woods*. We might assume that fifteen brief poems under such a title would derive from Indian poetry, poetry like the Ojibway song, for example, in which a warrior called Butterfly says:

                    In the coming heat
                    Of the day
                    I stood there.
                    (from A. Grove Day, *The Sky Clears*, p. 157)

The strength of his song, at least in translation, is from its
whole concept rather than from any detail of its execution.
But Lewis was influenced instead by the Imagism which was
then barely ten years old, which gave her the chance to com-
pose through sensory detail alone. And indeed, her "Nightfall
among Poplars" stands well beside the best of the original
Imagist poems:

                    As light grew horizontal,
                    I, among bracken,
                    Felt the cold ripples
                    Among bracken stems.

                    The quick dry spider
                    Ran across my hand.

There are three kinds of horizontal movement here, the first
from the source of light and the second from water—ripples
duplicated, as it were, on a breeze: and each of them is indefi-
nite, edgeless, as contrasted with the third—the light but clear
impression of the spider. Or *is* it a contrast? As often with the
pure Imagist poem, you cannot be certain whether the author
wants you to register the similarity or the dissimilarity of the
sensations juxtaposed. Are we Indians, feeling the connection
between phenomena, or Anglos, noting the distinction between them? As it is, the little spider gives me a wonderful
frisson of unrelatedness; but I have no way of knowing that
Lewis doesn't want me to relate the spider's movement to that
of the wind ripples in the same way as the butterfly's immobil-
ity is related to the warrior's in the Ojibway song.

   There is no doubt at all, however, of the intent behind
"Meadow Grass," another short poem of the 1920s, in which
interrelation of plants

> lacing their roots, lacing
> The life of the meadow into a deep embrace,

of living with dead and living, is echoed in the music of the
poem itself, rhyme lacing with rhyme both internal and terminal. In a magnificent recent poem too, "Comment in Passing,"
there is another kind of relation: we breathe in the ashes of
the dead, of the poisoner as of the loved one, so that "nothing
shall go to waste." Everybody, literally, becomes part of everybody else in this poem.

Nor is there any doubt of her intent when she writes the
"Words for a Song" of 1980, making use of a more daring
because more detailed analogy:

> Love is an anguish
> That, gathering at the root,
> Rises in sap along the rugged branch,
> Pulsing in sunlight,
> To lose itself in fruit.

It is difficult not to marvel at the firmness with which she links
love and the fruit tree, and the dexterity with which she
brings love's tears triumphantly up through the tree, a wetness of which the *vertu* engenders not only flower but fruit as
well.

3

Oliver Sacks, writing recently of Sign, the language of the
deaf, has said that "the beauty of language, and of Sign in
particular, is . . . that the concrete leads to the general, but *it is
through the general that one recaptures the concrete, intensified, transfigured.*"[1] In doing so, he inadvertently describes that special
kind of poetic maturing that took place in Janet Lewis's writing. In her earliest work, her grasp was on the specifics of the
tennis player or the spider, which Sacks calls the concrete; but
in "Meadow Grass" and "Words for a Song" her art has become complicated by the introduction of discursive elements:

thus concrete and general, image and concept, thing and idea, look both ways, each picking up strength from the other. Neither love nor fruit tree would be weak on its own, but it would be less alive. Such examples, it seems to me, render curiously irrelevant the debates about discourse versus image in the first part of this century. Love and tree need not be *versus* one another, they may work *in tandem*. They are connected as the lacing roots are connected. And when in another poem she relates the white oak to God, having it say

> In the long revery of life I stand
> Like Him who stirs forever in His thought,
> Yet moveth not,
> An image of Him in my constancy,
> An eldest child of God, the white oak tree,

the oak is referred to God, God is simultaneously referred to the oak, and the activity of each is made clearer to the reader. In her conception of God she recaptures the oak tree, "intensified and transfigured."

Recognizing and asserting continuity as she does in such poems, she is also able to identify discontinuity with especial sharpness. There are times, as with a fossil fern in which "the pattern stays, the substance gone," when there can no longer be such a fruitful exchange of energies. In the late 1920s she wrote a blank verse poem called "Country Burial." The coffin is laid by the grave's edge among grass and daisies, whose interlacing roots the corpse will soon join. To think of this is "comforting," as the idea of heaven is not:

> And this is comforting;
> For heaven is a blinding radiance where
> Leaves are no longer green, nor water wet,
> Milk white, soot black, nor winter weather cold,
> And the eyeless vision of the Almighty Face
> Brings numbness to the untranslatable heart.

Moving without apparent inconsistency from a gentle regret, Lewis defines heaven with a quiet, even unrelenting, tenacity. The living heart is untranslatable: if we shall meet in Paradise, we shall no longer be what we were, composed of attributes and loving the attributes of others. To speak in any other way would be falsification.

Death is interlaced with life, but it is not life's twin, not a wonderful Looking-Glass Land full of detached Rilkean presences. It is merely an absence, and as such demarcates, limits, and to that extent defines *by its abstraction* the very shape of the specific. A late poem, "Snail Garden," explains the way in which it does so:

> But I have taken sides in the universe.
> I have killed the snail that lay on the morning leaf
> . . . I have begun my day with death,
> Death given, death to be received.
> I have stepped into the dance.

As, in another poem, time is what creates music by defining it, so here death is what marks out the patterns of the dance, in which our steps approach and avoid, in which we give and receive. Thus she cannot conceive of life as an Imagist holiday: without the great abstractions of death and time there would be no specifics and no images for the attachments that we call love.

4

If the foregoing sounds schematic, that is my fault and not Janet Lewis's, and it is time to turn back to the poems as living wholes. In "The Clock," for example, the clock of the title starts as a conventional emblem of abstraction and is even juxtaposed with one of Lewis's dreamy gardens. What could be more cut-and-dried than that? But during the poem it comes to change places with the garden as focus of nostalgia: clock and garden move through the poem in a complicatedly changing relation, like that of the elaborate dance itself. Density of thought is expressed with lucid energy, and once again I am reminded of the initiating impulse, for what is behind the dance but the delighted and self-delighting body, of which the delicacy and vitality suggest the perceptions that they direct? The poem is a rich and generous achievement, and only one of many.

The anthologies will no doubt catch up with Janet Lewis. That they will does not justify the institution of the anthology, which is at best a convenience for teachers but otherwise a pernicious modern nuisance which keeps readers away from *books* of poetry. But it does raise the question of what you would name as, say, her five best poems. I would hesitate to do so, though I have been reading her for thirty-five years now. The pamphlet of 1988, *Late Offerings,* contain some of her freshest and most vigorous work. And now she is ninety: if she notices my words here, I would at least like to tell her that her poetry and her fiction mean more to me with each rereading.

NOTE

1. Oliver Sacks, *Seeing Voices* (Berkeley: University of California Press, 1989), p. 123, my italics.

Weedy Speech and Tangled Bank

Lorine Niedecker

It is appropriate that this last collection by Lorine Niedecker should be published, so attractively, in Britain, where more of her books appeared during her lifetime than in her own country. She was a little-known poet who toward the end of her rather hard and isolated life became the object of a cult. That was all to the good, in that cults may often keep difficult writers in print until the big public is ready for them. She was admired by certain poets among her contemporaries, none of *them* famous yet, and served a long sad faithful apprenticeship to Louis Zukofsky from a great distance. Her early poems especially, short and bare and awkward, tend to disconcert, looking, many of them, like amateur epigrams. But as you get used to them, you begin to recognize their specific kind of force. They are to epigrams somewhat as off-rhyme is to full rhyme—deriving their very authority from indirection and lack of neatness.

A poem like "Some float off on chocolate bars" is like a little essay: its brevities are as packed with meaning as with alliteration and assonance and other irregular resemblances in sound. If she lacks the epigrammatist's cutting assurance, her semblance of unpreparedness may make for a greater precision of statement: Kenneth Cox says it all when he describes her set-

---

Review of *Harpsichord and Salt Fish,* by Lorine Niedecker (Durham: Pig Press, 1991). Reprinted from *Times Literary Supplement,* February 14, 1992.

ting one thing alongside another "with the tremulous certainty of a compass needle."

Seeking relationship, in every sense, is her preoccupation. In an early short poem she refers to "our relative the air / [who] floods / our rich friend / silt"; in "Lake Superior," later and longer, she connects the iron in our blood with the ironwork on freighters; and she writes much about the literal ties of family. Her father was a carp-seiner in Northern Wisconsin who wanted her to work in a bank,

> but he'd given her a source
> to sustain her—
> a weedy speech,
> a marshy retainer.

She was interested in greener banks. It is not a flowered speech, then, but deliberately drab; and the ways of water are often a kind of model for her style, quirky, unpredictable, evasive, and transparent.

Her best poems, "In the great snowfall" or "The wild and wavy event," grow on you so that you can take her lamer efforts in your stride. The first of these, simple as it seems, is a cat's-cradle of allegiances, criss-crossed with the pull between public and private speech. The second is an example of a later development, being composed, Pound-like, largely out of extracts from the letters of John Adams: by her arrangements and her slight additions it becomes a complicated, surprising, and very touching original.

The three longer poems in *Harpsichord and Salt Fish* use this scrapbook method, on Jefferson, William Morris, and Darwin. Others have used it, but they always sound too much like Pound himself in their assemblings of documentary material. Only Niedecker, that I know of, recomposes her scraps into such fresh, sweet portraits.

This is a tiny book (even with its scholarly apparatus), of which the contents have already appeared elsewhere, but it is good to read it as the separate collection that the poet intended: as usual, it seems slight at first but responds to attention, taking on bulk with each rereading. Phrases start to grow on you: "Honest / Solid / The lip / of tipped / lily"; or (when Morris makes carpets by the river) "a long dream to unroll." The poem I especially enjoy is the last, on Darwin. He is a figure with whom she particularly sympathizes because, lonely like her, he finds a language in the natural world (as she inherited her weedy speech), and recognizes connection, relatedness, and kinship in a creation where details have been left "to the working of chance." They share a love of undergrowth, after all: her own consonants and vowels mutually entwined and supportive like the weeds in that famous tangled bank, in which all was interdependent.

Out of the Box
Elizabeth Bishop

Like other poets, John Ashbery and Mina Loy among them, Elizabeth Bishop was fascinated by the "boxes" of Joseph Cornell. In her final book she translated Octavio Paz's meditation about them. They are "hexahedrons of wood and glass, / scarcely bigger than a shoebox," and in them are arranged small *things,* many of them remarkable for their exquisite detail, and particularly things that are fragments of other things, "marbles, buttons, thimbles, dice / pins, stamps, and glass beads," assembled so as to form new wholes by association. The parallel to poetry is emphasized in what must surely be a conscious echo of Eliot when Bishop and Paz say to Cornell, "out of your ruins you have made creations."

The box then is a wonderful form, reminiscent of scrapbook, showcase, and children's game. "In the four corners of the box / shadowless ladies play at hide-and-seek." But if it resembles a poem too, it is not after all so similar to the wide distracted reach of *The Waste Land* as it is to the enclosed concentration of "The Mower to the Glowworms." Such a box or such a poem may be said to take unmanageable life and make it manageable by reducing it in scale—and the same might be said about a board game like Monopoly. It is oddly comforting in its containment, and yet just as oddly discomfiting in its implications of the excluded. It only hints at what

Review of *Becoming a Poet,* by David Kalstone (New York: Farrar, Straus & Giroux, 1989). First appeared as "In and Out of the Box," *Times Literary Supplement,* July 22–August 2, 1990.

cannot be contained within its limits—the dresses and suits that those pretty buttons come from, and their unattainable wearers.

My early impression of Elizabeth Bishop's own work was of this kind of poetry, determined as it always was by a longing for coziness, though a coziness often tinged with melancholy. Her first book, especially, displayed dazzling powers all the more remarkable for their limitation. The poems in it were like playthings, fresh-painted, decorative, charming, original, and yet tiny. She specialized, Alice-like, in altering the scale of things. "Cirque d'Hiver" was *about* a toy—a mechanical horse with a little dancer on its back. "The Man-Moth" and "Sleeping on the Ceiling" were only two of her childlike fantasies. "Seascape" was wittily personified, with the lighthouse "in black and white clerical dress" of a puritan preacher. No wonder she admired Paul Klee, whose world I once remember seeing unkindly characterized by John Richardson as, after all, rather *twee*. The same kind of thing continued in the second book, *A Cold Spring*, in the first poem of which I found:

> Now, from the thick grass, the fireflies
> begin to rise:
> up, then down, then up again:
> lit on the ascending flight,
> drifting simultaneously to the same height,
> —exactly like the bubbles in champagne.

The observation was exquisite, and apt; but somehow its cleverness seemed to be an end in itself. The images certainly lacked the bite of those in another fantasy, Mina Loy's "Lunar Baedeker," where for example "A flock of dreams / browse on Necropolis." And such self-absorbed playfulness approached inanity in later poems of that second book like "Letter to N.Y." and "Invitation to Miss Marianne Moore."

Her fifth book, *Geography III*, appeared in 1976, three years before her death, and here, all at once, everything was changed. Its longest three poems were directly concerned with uncontainable, unboxable experience. It was only ten poems long, and yet its achievement was such that it retrospectively altered the emphasis and shape of an entire career.

My mistake had been a common one, to look for a poet's best poetry among her typical work; and it was not to be found there any more than Hardy's is among "Satires of Circumstance." I could now see that all along she had been aware of the dangers of what attracted her. In "The Armadillo" she herself had said, of her own writing, I think: "too pretty, dreamlike mimicry!," and she could write disquieting, daringly messy poems as early as "Roosters" and as late as "Visits to St. Elizabeths." When I reread "Squatter's Children," its sad ingenuities reminded me of those in "Fear no more the heat o' the sun." And how could I have overlooked "At the Fishhouses"?

This last poem is about the human being on the land and the absolute nonhumanness of the sea, and about what mediates, in a sense, between them—the fish with their scales like sequins, and the seal "like me a believer in total immersion." There is a perfect balance between the playfulness of such images and the gravity of the poem's conclusion, which treats of the sea both as alien and at the same time something we must try to relate to: like an important abstraction, like "knowledge." The writing here achieves a positive grandeur:

> If you tasted it, it would first taste bitter,
> then briny, then surely burn your tongue.
> It is like what we imagine knowledge to be:
> dark, salt, clear, moving, utterly free,
> drawn from the cold hard mouth
> of the world, derived from the rocky breasts
> forever, flowing and drawn, and since
> our knowledge is historical, flowing, and flown.

In its brave uncompromising bleakness it reminds me a little of Marianne Moore's conclusion to one of her most splendid early poems, "A Grave." They are each writing about the sea, but making different distinctions about it: if there is indeed any debt to Moore here, it is not to be found in the detail but in a tone suggestive of a whole attitude toward experience.

The relation between Bishop and Moore is a famous one, and it is taken up in the first part of *Becoming a Poet*, by David Kalstone. Kalstone died leaving an incomplete manuscript, but Robert Hemenway's editorship is such that you would never guess it. (The book concludes with an "Afterword" by James Merrill, on Bishop's last poetry—but Merrill wisely does not attempt to emulate Kalstone-and-Hemenway's work, instead *suggesting* what might have been added, in a fragmentary and rather hesitant form.) The book is about the ways Bishop's work was affected by her two great literary friendships, with Moore and Robert Lowell; and it also, necessarily, traces some of the effect of Bishop on Lowell's work. It deals thoroughly with the whole subject of personal influence on poetry, in all the stages of a poem's conception and composition. Kalstone's reading of the obviously copious archives is balanced, sensitive, and responsible. He is more intent, you feel, on the accuracy of the record than in getting a good story—but he ends up with a good story anyway. I have read few books in which psychological and critical insight collaborate so well. It is, I would say, an immediate classic, not only for its success as a specific study but for its general implications about the complicated interactions between life and letters.

We first find Bishop, very young, in the role of apprentice to Moore—of apprentice but also, as Kalstone puts it, of "forward niece" who, though for four years she submitted her writing for "correction" by both Marianne Moore and her mother, had ideas of her own and would be able to recognize the point at which she had outgrown her tutelage. Meanwhile Moore's example was indispensable, and her advice was often the best possible. "I can't help wishing you would sometime in some way risk some unprotected profundity of experience," she wrote to Bishop about a short story, but the remark applies just as well to the poetry. Protection is what a box provides; and "unprotected profundity of experience" is exactly what she was to achieve in "At the Fishhouses."

But the climax and turning point of the Moores' influence had already been reached when Bishop sent them a typescript of "Roosters." It was a daring and idiosyncratic poem, a deliberate departure. John Berryman xeroxed it for his classes twenty years later, admiring it perhaps for its very instabilities—of image, of rhythms, of structure, even of rhyme. It has a graceful roughness, as of a ballet dancer playing a drunk; but its grace is far from contained or protected. Referring in it to Peter's betrayal of Christ, she says: "Old holy sculpture / could set it all together / in one small scene," but *she* chooses not to, and her scene opens up or narrows unpredictably. The Moores reacted by rewriting the poem extensively and sent it back to her, and their version, of great interest, appears here as an appendix. As Kalstone says, they tried in it "to keep the poem at a uniform satiric distance from its subject," restoring the very decorum that Bishop had for once set out to ignore.

After this, she removed herself to a perceptibly greater distance from mother and daughter. She remained their warm friend until their deaths, but talent has to be remorseless in the way it gets its nourishment: it eats and runs. Kalstone emphasizes that Bishop had already got what she needed from Moore in learning how to observe sensory detail, and she continued to value the older poet's "secure bravado in dealing with the physical world," but her own poems "increasingly dealt with the crises of observer and observed." The physical world, though it was closely described in Moore's fashion, was to have a different importance in her own writing. Speaking of her autobiographical work, Kalstone puts it happily:

> In the potentially shattering moments of these pieces about Bishop's early life, the girl's attention and feelings are constitutionally *deflected* from unsettling events. Objects hold radiant interest for her precisely because they help her absorb numbing or threatening experiences—the loon in ["First Death in Nova Scotia"] or the shop window and the blacksmith's in "In the Village."

Since they had "radiant interest" in themselves, there was no temptation to turn them into symbols, filling up with meaning. And so we come, by contraries, to Robert Lowell, one of whose great talents was indeed that of loading the physical world with his own meanings. He is quoted as saying of "At the Fishhouses," "I'm a fisherman myself, but all my fish become symbols, alas." In a late poem to Bishop, describing her slow, painstaking, and tentative methods of composition, he says (and Merrill quotes it aptly in his Afterword):

> Have you seen an inchworm crawl on a leaf,
> cling to the very end, revolve in air,
> feeling for something to reach something? . . .

The identification between the caterpillar's activity and the poet's is nothing less than brilliant, and by example serves to point to the crucial difference between his and her attitudes toward the image, which implies an even larger difference between their poetries. Hers derived through Moore from the Ruskinian-Imagist belief that the world out there was adequate in itself—something to be respected and reproduced as accurately as possible; his was the imperial attitude of, say, Yeats, that it is there to be used, to have meanings imposed on it or read into it, to be interpreted by the poet according to need. The imperial poet is not modest: Lowell wanted in his political poetry to be the conscience of his time, in his "imitations" to be the transmitter of past culture, and in his personal poetry to be the representative poetic consciousness working through exemplary private materials. Bishop, on the other hand, was by choice and temperament a more passive poet. "Bishop's particularizing, accurate character was always a challenge to Lowell's mythmaking, his way of noting things with a generosity or obliquity or malice just on the edge of fiction," says Kalstone. Thus the two of them noted and appreciated their differences—even relished them, for a long time—and I heard each of them refer to the other without qualification as "my best friend, of course."

Though they were the opposites who attracted, their friendship did not finally change them so much as help them toward a completer awareness of their own potentialities. Bishop's "The Armadillo" led Lowell to his "Skunk Hour," and her autobiographical stories showed him what he could do in first the prose and then the poetry of *Life Studies*, which in turn gave her the idea of linking poems about her Brazilian experience.

And yet their differences did come to matter, a great deal. She was increasingly distressed by what she was coming to see as Lowell's appropriations. He was no longer just imposing meanings on things, but stealing and distorting human utterances so as to dramatize them for his own ends. Thus, she tried to keep him closer to the originals of some Rimbaud poems he was turning into English. Not that it mattered *that* much: after all, Rimbaud's poetry was available in French and would continue to hold its own. But the situation was more serious when Lowell appropriated the language of the living. In one poem he used a private letter from herself, written in emotional distress; and in others he used letters from Elizabeth Hardwick, his second wife, unhappy, brave, and vulnerable, addressed to him from New York while he was embarking on his third marriage in England.

In his transcriptions from private correspondence so as to make it part of Lowellian mythology, Bishop found two betrayals. One was of the person whose words were used, being in effect a brutal violation of personal trust; and the other was of the reader, who had no control text, no French original, to check for the distortions and omissions and changes of emphasis that he made. Kalstone projects the difference in their attitudes even farther, saying that the real contrast between them is in the way they think of guilt. "Lowell's conviction was that the written word could convey and explore it; Bishop's settled position was that writing countered it, challenged energies in new and healing directions. 'In general, I deplore "the confessional,"' she had written him," and we are told elsewhere that "she disliked W. D. Snodgrass's *Heart's Needle* [which Lowell had praised] for its self-congratulatory 'I do all these awful things but don't you think I'm really nice.'"

The argument was conducted, largely by letter, in careful and courteous terms. Bishop and Lowell were aware of the importance they had for each other, and it wasn't just literary. So, although feelings ran deep, and the problem was not resolved, they remained friends. And indeed theirs is a fine instance of a friendship between poets; they treated each other as equals, and I do not think, considering them at this distance, that they were after all poets so disproportionate in achievement.

This last remark may surprise, for during their lives Lowell always had a topical edge over Bishop, but the passing of time has now taken it from him. Perhaps he started with greater gifts than she, he certainly wrote far more, and he was more ambitious. There are things in his work that stick in the mind, and will continue to, I hope: the modernized *Lycidas*-music of "The Quaker Graveyard in Nantucket," the image of the dogged skunk at the end of "Skunk Hour," and the masterly linking of the personal with the political in "Waking Early Sunday Morning." Though he was capable of stylistic sloppiness scarcely credible in a professional poet, though he dramatized himself endlessly and tediously, and though much of his poetry is simply high-brow journalism, he was on occasion capable of turning his unremitting restlessness into some fine declamatory poetry, in the teeth of its own flamboyance, as it were. But it is worth suggesting that Bishop's greater evenness of vision and her sense of responsibility toward a world to be lived in and not conquered enabled her in the end to write poetry that, in its quiet, seemingly offhand, but emphatic way, may do more for us than the most resounding of Lowell's hair-raising exploits.

With such thoughts in mind, we might consider her late poem "The Moose." Three-quarters of it consists of little else besides images of containment: the tides domesticated, lupins like apostle spoons, bumble bees inside foxgloves, a dog tucked in her shawl at night, small picture following small picture. Yet though the images and groups of images are neatly enclosed, they are not also separated like Cornell's boxes; rather, they are connected like the houses in a friendly village. Lewis Carroll and Paul Klee are both now worlds away, and the feeling is less of coziness than of family comfort. Stepping back from the poem a bit, we may see the continuing implied effect of *connected units*, individuals to families, families to villages, villages to a whole rural Nova Scotia, part dependent on part. These are the ways we might connect ourselves in a simple and sensible society, by sharing a language or a bus or a whole fabric of memories. It all holds equally together.

And the moose comes out from "the impenetrable wood." By making the obvious contrast with Frost's magnificently real-zed buck in "The Most of It," we may see that, interestingly enough, the moose is hardly presented to us at all—it is suggested, rather, a huge presence not completely *taken in* (for it does remain outside). Though there is a moment of rare charm in the way "it sniffs at / the bus's hot hood," it's as if it is too extraordinary to be translated into the terms of the small society on the bus. It cannot be appropriated—cannot be contained in language any more than in symbol or box—and the fact that it can't is what gives those in the bus a "sweet / sensation of joy," a release into something other than themselves so great that they still hanker for it after they have driven on.

> For a moment longer,
>
> by craning backward,
> the moose can be seen
> on the moonlit macadam;
> then there's a dim
> smell of moose, an acrid
> smell of gasoline.

The humans are returned to their usual category, somewhere between gasoline and moose, but they sense that they have gone as completely beyond those accepted limits as if they had met an angel.

The same feeling of release is to be found, on a tiny scale, in what appears to have been Bishop's last poem, "Sonnet":

> Caught—the bubble
> in the spirit-level,
> a creature divided;
> and the compass needle
> wobbling and wavering,
> undecided.
> Freed—the broken
> thermometer's mercury
> running away;
> and the rainbow-bird
> from the narrow bevel
> of the empty mirror,
> flying wherever
> it feels like, gay!

She ends her career on an enviable note. It is her finest piec
of playfulness, celebrating a deliverance from reductions an
enclosures even as it delights in the very restrictions of for
that make its utterance possible, Ariel forever preserved i
the process of being freed from his Prospero-box.

Small Persistent Difficulties

Robert Creeley

Popular though Robert Creeley's poetry has become in recent years, its language has never fit in with the official current notions of the poetic. For example, the verbs do not work harder than, say, the adjectives; there is as little metaphor as in the most straightforward prose; and the diction throughout tends to be general, being unsuited to the sensory effects we prize nowadays. So much for the orthodoxies of the twentieth century, Creeley might remark, but I am left trying to reconcile my conviction that poetry does work primarily through the vigor of its language with my experience that *his* poetry does speak to me, and to many others, in a way I find powerful and persuasive.

How does his language work, then? In commenting on the neutrality of Creeley's diction, one poet has evoked the name of Waller, and another has compared his pared-down anti-rhetorical flatness to the plain style of an early Elizabethan like Barnabe Googe. Nor do you have to go far to pick up Renaissance echoes: here is a poem from about 1960 called "For Friendship":

> For friendship
> make a chain that holds,
> to be bound to
> others, two by two,

Review of *Collected Poems, 1945–1975*, by Robert Creeley (Berkeley: University of California Press, 1982). Reprinted from *Times Literary Supplement*, November 4, 1983.

> a walk, a garland,
> handed by hands
> that cannot move
> unless they hold.

Neither Waller nor Googe are inappropriate names to connect with this sweet-natured and sweet-sounding generalization, in which the complete neutrality of language exposes a density of definition, and if the sheer melody of Waller is not achieved (or even aimed at), it is in a sense glanced at by the tetrameters, which he both creates and at the same time carefully rejects in the lineation of the first stanza. The rejection of regularity, minute though it is here, already points to a great difference between Creeley's and any Renaissance practice. The poem reminisces about iambs but it has its own slightly shifted rhythm, which is sustained not by a tradition but by the varying pace of the singular voice.

If Creeley has come to dislike simile, finally, as "always a displacement of what *is* happening," he has come also to dislike all regularization, because it does something like the same thing. In a recent interview he said about Charles Tomlinson's use of the triadic line, which was invented late in life by William Carlos Williams, that Tomlinson was "missing where the initiating impulse is in Williams." It is all-important for him then to be true to what *is* happening, to stick to the initiating impulse, to keep from what he sees as the dead predictabilities of a systematized rhythm or language. Throughout his career I notice the recurring term of *stumbling* for his poetic procedure, most recently in the "Prayer to Hermes" (from *Later,* a collection not included in *Collected Poems*), in which he addresses the god,

> My luck
> is your gift,
> my melodious
> breath, my stumbling.

If one stumbles, led or pushed by impulse, one stumbles into the unforeseen, the accidental. Even so, the accidental may have its patterns. In a poem of more than twenty years ago, "For Love," he says:

> Let me stumble into
> not the confession but
> the obsession I begin with
> now . . .

A confession may be for once only, but an obsession recurs. However, it recurs as something felt afresh and with its original force: to adopt Lawrentian terms, you might say that it rises up again as a renewal and not a repetition. The poetics of impulse and renewed accident is closer to Lawrence's "poetry of the present" ("flexible to every breath," said Lawrence) than to the sententiae, or perhaps cynical epigrams, of Googe's beautiful poem "Of Money."

It was Creeley who made the famous remark that form is never more than an extension of content, and insofar as the accidents of composition are embodied in the surviving poem, his remark is constantly illustrated, for he apparently does not tidy up the odd, the peculiar, or the awkward. His suggestive or at times puzzling strangeness is directly opposed to the calculations behind those kinds of rhetoric of which he has so much dread. There is for example the disconcerting language of the last lines to "The Whip": "for which act / I think to say this / wrongly," where because the reference of "this" is unclear and the locution "I think to" unusual, the whole poem is called in question: thus the characteristics of the style enter the content of the poem, as they always must.

Easy as Creeley's poetry looks at first glance, then, much of it is to be grasped only with the closest of attention. The *Collected Poems* is a formidable volume to read straight through: even though it stops short at 1975, thus omitting two later books published by New Directions, it is 671 agreeably printed pages long. You are lucky in fact if you have had the opportunities to read most of the work as it came out in the original collections over the last thirty years.

But certain general impressions strike me at once about his

career as a whole. The first is that the style does not go through any but quite minor changes from beginning to end. I find more of the wonderful comedy early on, and the most recent poetry of all (I am thinking of *Later*) has been hospitable to some dreadfully soft emotion about growing old, but essentially the poetry is still written with the same plain terse language and the same sure command over the verse movement. The next general tendency I notice is that there are changes in the organization of the poems volume by volume. The early poems are complete in themselves, independent of each other, however much they may share themes. In the collections of the 1970s, however, *Pieces* and *In London*, for example, poem leads into poem, group leads into group, and the book rather than the individual poem becomes the meaningful unit. There is also in these books far more fragmentary material included—what you might plausibly call notebook jottings, some of them interesting in connection with the rest of the work or with our thinking about Creeley, some of them less so. The poetics of accident may permit a stumble of this sort, entitled "Kid":

> "What are you doing?"
> Writing some stuff.
>
> "You a poet?"
> Now and then.

Form here is only too clearly an extension of content. I can afford to comment with a certain acerbity because my admiration is so great elsewhere: I want to warn the new reader who dips into the enormous book and pulls out this kind of thing before coming to the good writing. But it would be a mistake for any critic to train his great guns on such minimal poems; there are a large number of them altogether, exercises, notations, experiments, jokes, but I can't take them very seriously, either to like or dislike. After all, there is a certain proportion of deadness present in the complete collected works of any poet.

In one sense, though, "Kid" *is* a characteristic poem, from its very modesty. It is an epigram, of sorts. Creeley is at once to be differentiated from his old associates Olson and Duncan by the kind of poem he wants to write. Where their ambitions were epic, expansive, inclusive, drawing upon whole libraries of outside material, his were doggedly narrower, drawing almost entirely on the irregular pulse of the personal. This is not to say that he aims at the "lyric," even though he has entitled many a poem "Song," for with him it is the speaking voice that matters, not singing or lyring but stumbling, with all the appearance of improvisation, tentatively and unevenly moving forward, but with a singular gift of "melodious breath," a gift for the true-sounding measure that Williams himself once praised. (Before you accuse Creeley of speaking in cliché about his lines taking "the beat from the breath," you should remember that it was he and Olson who originated the phrase: it is not their fault that others stiffened it into platitude.) And his narrow subject matter, that field of energy through which he stumbles, is the intensely apprehended detail of the heterosexual private life.

The feeling in his best poetry is fresh and clean; as though it is discovering itself just as it gets written. Creeley takes nothing for granted, and if his doing so makes for the wonderful unexpected funniness of "I know a man," and for the hilarious lines in his serious troubadour poem "The Door," and for the lovely frankness of "Something," the poem about the pee-shy lover, it is also responsible for a depressed awareness of vulnerability like that illustrated in the note about going through New York in a taxi where he records his "continual sense of small . . . persistent difficulties." The vulnerability exposed in Creeley's poetry is almost constant. But nobody has ever pretended that stumbling was a fluid motion; it is, precisely, an encountering of small persistent difficulties in moving ahead, and if the phrase about New York describes one of the main subjects of his poetry it of course can be taken to refer to the style as well. Finally you could say that his strength arises from his constant perception of weakness. If he is the most heterosexual of poets he is also the least macho.

One situation you can find again and again in Creeley is that of the speaker in bed, either alone or not, uneasily lapsing in and out of sleep, in and out of dream. It occurs for example in a well-known poem, "The World," which starts:

> I wanted so ably
> to reassure you, I wanted
> the man you took to be me,
>
> to comfort you, and got
> up, and went to the window,
> pushed back, as you asked me to,
>
> the curtain, to see
> the outline of the trees
> in the night outside.

To hear a reading by Creeley at his best is to be aware of the importance he gives to line-endings. He makes a point of pausing on them *always*, whether there is punctuation or not: his free verse line is thus always preserved as an audibly identified unit. The result is a kind of eloquent stammering; there is a sense of small persistent difficulties all right, but of each being overcome in turn, while it occurs—the voice hesitates, and then plunges forward. You can see how such a reading suits the above lines, with what kind of obstinate holding-on it must stumble forward, even past the interruption, the almost pushed-in qualification, of "as you asked me to," and finally getting there, to the end of the sentence, having thus *felt* its way through the poem's opening. The movement forward in these lines is certainly as much part of the meaning as the language itself, which as usual is plain in the extreme. Plain yet not always obvious: "ably" makes a point of much subtlety about the kind of firm flexibility he would have if he were the man she took him to be. And that third line, a breath-unit in itself, implies a large and complicated statement about assumptions and appearances. I want to go on to quote the rest of the poem, taking it in two more parts, not only because it is one of Creeley's best but because once you have come to terms with it you have made an entry into all of his work by discovering the comprehensiveness of packed life beneath the apparently simple and prosaic surface. It is a bare scene indeed: nothing much physical has been seen with clarity, nothing much has been done. An outline of trees is visible, that is all, because a curtain has been pushed back. But an outline of certain feelings has also been suggested, and that gives us something to go on when we embark on the long second sentence:

> The light, love,
> the light we felt then,
> greyly, was it, that
>
> came in, on us, not
> merely my hands or yours,
> or a wetness so comfortable,
>
> but in the dark then
> as you slept, the grey
> figure came so close
>
> and leaned over,
> between us, as you
> slept, restless, and
>
> my own face had to
> see it, and be seen by it,
> the man it was, your
>
> grey lost tired bewildered
> brother, unused, untaken—
> hated by love, and dead,
>
> but not dead, for an
> instant, saw me, myself
> the intruder, as he was not.

It is a sentence so thick with comma-enclosed qualifications, because so much is happening simultaneously, that you can easily lose yourself in it. But the remedy is in your voice: it is even truer of Creeley than of most poets that the way to understand him is to learn how to read him aloud. From testing one reading against another you can "feel out" what it is "we felt" that ties the first part of the sentence together. We felt not merely each other's hands, not merely the wetness (of orgasm, it must be), but the grey light which in dream vision congeals to the ghost of the dead brother. Such exploration with the voice shows the density of the sentence to be wonderfully justified: it is not sensory writing in the usual way, not like Tennyson or Hart Crane, but it is as if, rather, Creeley goes directly to the organs that do the sensing. Synesthesia occurs casually and as a matter of course. And the greyness when it comes the third time has become a quality of being— for the grey brother who lived in some limbo, where he still momentarily persists, was "unused, untaken": his greyness, his indefiniteness was such that "the world" had no use for him at all, it did not even exploit him! The reading voice (mine, yours, not necessarily Creeley's) continues, interrupting itself, but resuming, into a further change. The ghost intruder for an instant looks on me, the speaker, as the intruder there in the bed. That is the man *he* takes me to be. By comparison with him even I seem "able"—competent, fluent, potent—belonging as I do to the world of the living. The pathos is far-reaching.

> I tried to say, it is
> all right, she is
> happy, you are no longer
>
> needed. I said,
> he is dead, and he
> went as you shifted
>
> and woke, at first afraid,
> then knew by my own knowing
> what had happened—
>
> and the light then
> of the sun coming
> for another morning
> in the world.

The last line would perhaps be weak if "the world," though not referred to as such before this, had not picked up so much weight of meaning during the poem as a whole. The world here is the real world with its commonsense light contrasting to the grey light of the love-making and the ghost: but wasn't it also the place that produced the brother, that rejected him so thoroughly before his death? The reassurance of the new day is tempered by the implication that we are creating our own ghosts of deprivation and despair as we go about our lives.

I find this poem characteristic of Creeley at his best. He has gone beyond, or behind, the classic twentieth-century split between image and discourse: he does not attempt sharpness of physical image, and the discursive part of the poetry is more aptly termed "assertion" (the word used of it by Robert Pinsky, the poet who compared him to Googe). Though "The World" takes a narrative form it is like many of Creeley's nonnarrative poems in that the real course it follows is that of the mind, wandering, but at the same time trying to focus in on its own wandering and to map a small part of its course accurately and honestly, however idiosyncratic that course may seem to be—idiosyncratic in its pace, in its syntax, even in its subject matter. In attuning our voices to that mind, in paying our full attention to the way it moves and shifts, we become part of its own attentiveness and can share in "the exactitude of his emotion."

It is by that sharing that the apparent idiosyncrasy ceases to be such, that is ceases to be special or unique. Creeley himself has the best comment here, on the opening page of the introduction to his Penguin selection from Whitman: "It is, paradoxically, the personal which makes the common in so far as it recognizes the existence of the many in the one. In my own joy or despair, I am brought to that which others have also experienced."

Living in the Present
Donald Hall

"REAL LIFE ROCK, TOP TEN." I read it in the *Village Voice* last January, compiled by the music critic Greil Marcus—a list of heterogeneous items linked by their energy and their iconoclasm, the characteristics of rock 'n' roll. And Number One (just above Keith Richards live in Oakland) was "Prophecy," a ranting curse out of sixty-year-old Donald Hall's *The One Day,* a book-length poem.

> Your children will wander looting the shopping malls
> for forty years, suffering for your idleness,
> until the last dwarf body rots in a parking lot
> . . . the sky will disappear like a scroll rolled up,

Marcus quotes and compares the prophetic voice to that of the early Dylan, of Isaiah, of Johnny Rotten, "defining what rock 'n' roll no longer dares to say." Something about Hall's poetry has always made it timely, a part of the news as well as of literature.

He started, like most writers, embedded in the idiom of his time. It was the 1950s, and his early, prize-winning poems were about exile and existential estrangement. Holding his newborn child in his arms, he addressed it as "my son, my executioner"; he mourned the decay of rural New Hampshire, where he had spent his school vacations; and he de-

---

Review of *The One Day,* by Donald Hall (New York: Ticknor and Fields, 1988). First appeared as "The Late Spring of Donald Hall," *Los Angeles Times Book Review,* November 5, 1989.

tailed the dull familiar features of the suburbia in which he had been raised. Those almost identical "dark houses harden into sleep," he wrote, and it was a sleep where he saw no refreshment, no waking into vigor.

But he was looking for something more. Searching for an imagery equivalent to the heartland from which we have been exiled, he entered next upon a different kind of poetry. In "The Long River" he rows into a dark, mysterious interior:

> The musk-ox smells
> in his long head
> my boat coming.

The musk-ox is both ominous and vital: his appetites have become forgotten in suburbia. The spondaic phrases give the writing a slowness, a weight, that it has not had before. And its syllabic form—Hall was the inventor of syllabics in our time—makes for a more unpredictable verse movement than in the earlier poetry, with which it has little in common.

It was now the 1960s, and he moved into different kinds of free verse. "The Alligator Bride" embodies a kind of jocular surrealism. Such investigations of the irrational, however, led him eventually to the true sources of the rural nostalgia that had always haunted him. He quit teaching at Ann Arbor in 1975, remarried, and moved back to the farmhouse of his maternal grandparents, not as farmer himself but as a writer who wanted to raise poetry on farmland. And he succeeded, writing poems less elegies for the past than realizations of it—about the cart-horses and the henyard, the Holsteins and the ox-cart man—their lives thick with things: he lifted the recurrent rhythms of the farming year into the present tense.

His career seemed inconsistent and unpatterned, as Herman Melville's must have looked during his time, or Shakespeare's. But he was always consistent in his subject matter, his poetry being preoccupied with the shared rather than the exceptional experience, with what we have or could have in common.

Thus *The One Day* consists of the voices of all of us. The poem is in three parts. The first opens with an aging man daydreaming and smoking in his yellow chair, "unfit / to work or love." His voice is joined by a woman's, but they are the same voice though they speak of different lives, and we come to understand that they have led the same life, in which the promise of fullness has been answered only by the fact of emptiness. They speak of a self without center, an existence without revelation or joy. "The world is a bed," they say; that is, the world has become reduced to a bed of adultery, a bed of insomnia, a bed of sleep only after pills chased down with whiskey. The voices weave and alternate, but they speak of the same dead end: of having been unwillingly herded into a present with no real connection to past or future, a present in which they find neither rest nor meaning.

It is written in a line based on the Old English accentual line as it was loosened and revised by Pound, one of the most useful and flexible technical innovations of the century. The collage and juxtaposition of experience that he uses is also a modified Poundian method, making possible the economical inclusion of a great deal of specific heterogeneous material.

For this poem is all detail and circumstance, the one day made up of many specific days, the one life of many lives, though they lead the speaker into the same narrow place, at the end of which is only fear. At the end of the first part the female voice tells, with a deadly flatness, how she prepares to give her children pills which will kill them. Then there enters

> someone whose identity hovers just out of sight, the way
> a beekeeper's mask darkens a face,

who picks up a rag doll and starts to demonstrate on it the proper ways to dismember a child, as one might a dead fowl, by cutting its limbs carefully into sections.

Though Part One ends thus in nightmare, it has been moderate in tone, that of someone no longer possessing the energy to direct his or her own life. By contrast, Part Two, with the title "Four Classic Texts," starts with rage. "Prophecy," which reminded Greil Marcus of Johnny Rotten, is a curse—against our civilization and against life itself. It is succeeded by the rage of satire, a bitter satire of love and sex and marriage, in "Pastoral."

The world is still a bed, in which "we pull off our clothes like opening junk mail." "History" follows, rage against the past, and consists of a terrible parody of what already parodies itself, the list of human destructiveness, and Tiberius melts into Stalin. The fourth classic text, though, is not like the others: "Eclogue" replaces their destructive rage with its opposite extreme—a visionary certainty, the return to an age of gold through a cyclical process in which we recapture innocence, "the vector of greed withdraws," and there is a "restitution of lost things."

We are to make what we will of this middle section. The "Four Classic Texts" are thrust between Parts One and Three, and we must supply the connection for ourselves. What I think is implied is that his composite protagonist has been moved out of the earlier quiet and rational despair into a full-bodied irrationality, of crazy angers and equally crazy hope, which are at least signs of energy, of not surrendering to the presence with the darkened face.

So that when in the last part we return to the original speakers, though they are still old and in the same world, they are changed—*enabled*. The brushes with craziness have released them from their inertia. They still live in the present, but now they live in it fully. No longer "unfit / to work or love," they now find joy in both.

> When my body shook again with the body's passion,
> it was possible only because I expected nothing.

And a proposition is reversed—in a kind of echo of John Donne's "The Sun Rising": "a bed is the world," inclusive, and receptive to possibilities. The polysyllabic ironies from earlier in the poem are replaced by praise, not only of blossoms and old lilacs, but of "fried Spam and onions on slices of Wonder Bread."

What Hall achieves in this third part is an extraordinarily complex presentation of the grounds for joy, difficult enough to describe at any time, a joy that has nothing in common with complacency, for it is active, intelligent, and completely aware that it is to be ended by death, which in fact helps to define it.

The rage and satire have been worked off, but the promise of a cyclical return is in its way kept.

> On the first Sunday of every month we assemble
> molecules of Jesus from their diaspora,

he says, while a few lines farther down

> When the rain drives on the poppies they hold bright
> petals to the rain.

Raindrops recur and disappear, as the molecules of Jesus disappear and recur. There is one day: past and future are contained in the present of the one day as the whole world is contained in the one bed. Everything is present at the same time:

> The tomcat
> plays with his mother, sucking and teasing; he cuffs
> his mother's jaw. The tomcat limps home in the bloody
> morning, ear torn. The tomcat sleeps all day
> in a portion of sun, fur tatty over old scars, pulls
> himself to the saucer of milk, and snores going back
> to sleep, knowing himself the same. The kitten leaps
> in the air, her paws spread like a squirrel's.

The beauty of this writing is not merely in what it says, that the stages of our lives are in some way coexistent, but in the way it so actively *is* what it says, in the specifics of the cat and in the pacing of those specifics. The joy and the acceptance are neither glib nor unexamined.

Among his numerous prose books, Hall has written at least one, *Remembering Poets* (1978), which is of permanent value, not only for its observant memoirs of Dylan Thomas, Frost, Eliot, and Pound, but for the brilliant way he moves from them into his reflections about the nature of poetry itself. He says "poetry attempts . . . to add old or irrational elements to the light of consciousness by means of language, which is the instrument of consciousness." The poet thus adds unreason to reason, "making a third thing." It seems to me that this describes well what Hall has done in *The One Day:* mere reason was combined with mere irrationality and the two in combination produce the refined and alert awareness, the late spring, of the third part, a life going through the same processes as a poetry.

And this poem, as a whole, may indeed be seen as the synthesis of a whole life's work. It is one of those books, like Elizabeth Bishop's last collection, which alters the way we look at the jumbled contents of the poetic career preceding it, giving it retrospectively a shape, a pattern, a consistency it didn't seem to have at the time.

A Record

Allen Ginsberg's Poetry

There is still a feeling around, though it is less common than it was, that Allen Ginsberg is not quite—well *you* know, isn't he perhaps more of a *public figure* than a *poet*? Some won't even grant him that importance: a few years ago J. D. McClatchy wrote of him, at the PEN Congress, as an "overly familiar, and by now rather tacky, figure at such gatherings," language that certainly startled me for its open contemptuousness, even though the critic added, patronizingly enough, "but I give him credit for honesty." Honesty, so grudgingly conceded, is evidently a secondary virtue. Though it may have been his conduct that produced this particular response (heckling the Secretary of State and carrying a petition that supported the embattled Nicaraguan government), Ginsberg's life and his writing have always been of a piece, and since bad taste and honesty have indeed marked his poetry from the start, it is a whole career that is being sneered at.

Yet good taste has never had any necessary connection with poetry, certainly not with that of the poets Ginsberg has taken as models. Whitman offended almost all his contemporaries with his sexual references, whether perfectly understood by them or not, and there are lines and passages in

Reprinted from *European Gay Review* 5 (1989) and *James White Review* 8, no. 4. I merely scrape the edge of Ginsberg's politics, which Gregory Woods discusses fully in his beautifully written chapter on Ginsberg in his *Articulate Flesh*. One section of that chapter is entitled "The Sexuality of Politics."

Leaves of Grass which might be said to triumph through their very tastelessness: "I dote on myself, there is that lot of me and all so luscious" is funny because outrageous, and being funny and outrageous it is appropriate, it is not out of place, it is part of the great inclusive statement made by "Song of Myself." And Blake, in his entirely different way, was also a master of offensiveness.

Blake, however, had a minuscule public; and even Whitman didn't have to deal with the scale of the notoriety that Ginsberg suddenly achieved at the age of thirty. Fame is difficult for a writer to deal with—impossible to disregard, it dries you up, or it makes you think you are infallible, or your writing becomes puffed out with self-esteem. (Victor Hugo thought himself superior to both Jesus and Shakespeare.) It is a complication that the imagination can well do without. "Some fantasy of Fame / I dreamt in adolescence Came true last week on television," remarks Ginsberg in 1977, and in truth adolescent fantasies of fame were coming true from the publication of *Howl* onward. Ginsberg responded to it all with characteristic good sense—since he couldn't reject fame, he wouldn't try to, but he wasn't going to value it for any more than it was worth, which was not much: he treated it as simply a fact in his life, and it became another piece of subject matter like his sexuality, his childhood in Paterson, the America he lives in. There is a short and modest poem of his from 1969, called "After Thoughts," in which he makes love, with a male of course, and afterwards describes himself

> Mirror looking, combing
>   gray glistening beard
> Were I found sharp eyed
>   attractive to the young?
> Bad magic or something—
> Foolish magic most likely.

Foolish magic, that is exactly what fame is. The poem of which I have quoted the second part is a mere casual notation perhaps, but it stayed firmly in my mind for many years before I came across it again, for its "sharp eyed" attentiveness to the comic possibilities in its subject matter, and for its choice to avoid the easier attitudes of cynicism or romanticism. In its small way, it may be taken as a kind of paradigm of Ginsberg's poetry.

A poet with better taste would not have touched the subject, I suspect, or would have taken it up only to falsify it into some kind of elegance, but Ginsberg is plainly drawn by its very intractibility, by the built-in inelegance which in a way may be considered to validate it, to make it authentic. (In his attraction to inherently awkward material, Ginsberg resembles Hardy.) Moreover, he is interested in observation, and in accurate observation, and the desire for accuracy, I would say, *is* a prerequisite of poetry—because if the poet does not endeavour to tell the truth as he observes it, then his poetry becomes simply a piece of decoration. The "honesty" allowed him by our little Lord Chesterfield is at the root of all Ginsberg's poetry, if you interpret honesty as an attempt at faithfulness to the record, public or private, literal or imaginative. To read through the 746 pages of his *Collected Poems 1947–1988* and the subsequent volume *White Shroud* feels a bit like progressing through an exceptionally frank and full autobiography. You are impressed by the truthfulness and detail of the record: and the inspiring mind is besides so interesting, playing as it does on such a variety of material.

There are plenty of verifiable facts to chew over in this record, and if the writing is at intervals tedious and even foolish, it is only so as any good friend's conversation may be on his off days, and I would not want to take those days otherwise than in the context of a whole life, which I have come to trust. Much of the physical detail making up that life is unforgettable: his Aunt Rose is well known, but there is a whole company of swiftly and accurately delineated minor figures besides. Here is one:

> Eat Eat said the sign, so I went in the Spanish Diner
> The girl at the counter, whose yellow Bouffant roots
>   grew black over her pinch'd face,
>   spooned her coffee with knuckles

                    puncture-marked,
        whose midnight wrists had needletracks,
               scars inside her arms:
       "Wanna go get a Hotel Room with me?"

She "spooned her coffee": her whole activity is summed up in
the verb, but also it is his concentration on her hands which
leads to the observation of the needle tracks, and his concentration once remarked by her leads to her question. She is
there in herself, and like Aunt Rose and Neal Cassady and
Ginsberg's mad mother Naomi she is exactly placed in the
immense and fascinating enclosing narrative implied by the
Collected Poems, a background figure to be sure whereas they
are major characters, but one who in her very helpless brevity
has a representative weight—in the total experience, in the
memory, in the America Ginsberg tries to comprehend.

   This autobiography has everything, facts, characters, and
many a story too, from the long agonizing narrative in *Kaddish*
of the years with Naomi down to the painful and memorable
anecdotes of "Uptown" and "Imaginary Universes"—bare little tales of an encounter with a "hatted lean citizen" leaving a
bar and of another with a "Mexican faced boy, 19 / in Marine
cloth" on a plane trip. To each of these anecdotes there is a
frankly didactic purpose, and Ginsberg is in fact a moralist as
insistent and as impassioned as, for example, D. H. Lawrence.
He has written what I consider the best political poetry in
English of the last thirty years. It is of great variety. Many have
remarked that *Howl* is delivered in the manner of a prophet, a
Dada Jeremiah perhaps. By the time he comes to *Wichita Vor-
tex Sutra* he is writing a more conventional political poetry,
explicit and factual, in which he uses the *Cantos* as rhetorical
models, learning from them how best to dispose a great deal
of factual material on the page. His most persuasive political
poetry, however, is indirect. The junkie-girl at the counter is
an example of it: her very presence tells us something, implicitly, about the state of America.

   Ginsberg writes from no political party. His masters are
those poets who have found divinity in the human body

rather than the State. His first book had as epigraph, moreover, those lines in which Whitman most sounds like the Blake
of *The Marriage of Heaven and Hell:*

> Unscrew the locks from the doors!
> Unscrew the doors themselves from the jambs!

a call for the breaking down of barriers, and for an openness
of style and content, that I wish had stayed at the beginning of
his works as epigraph to the whole lot, rather than being
relegated as it has been to an appendix. Ginsberg may have
sympathized with the Sandinistas, but that does not make him
a Marxist. He is an anarchist: a polysexual Blakean anarchist
with distinct tendencies toward Whitmanian homosexual democracy, which are in turn offset by early dealings with visionary Dada. (I think that gets it all in.) This is the Ginsberg who
frankly found the handsome Che Guevara an *erotic* figure
and who was kicked out of Czechoslovakia because he aspired
to the principle of orgy, which is subversive to every authorita-
tive State, perhaps to the idea of the State itself. After all, it is
the road of excess, not of obedience and discipline, that leads
to the palace of wisdom.

The impulse toward anarchy is the source of his politics, his
eroticism, and also of his humor. Though he has probably not
written one entirely comic poem (in the sense that "The English Are So Nice!" is a comic poem), it is Ginsberg's humor,
occurring often in the most serious of situations, that constitutes the distinguishing effect of his poetry. The professor picking his nose, the bard with semen on his beard, these are the
rueful self-portrayals at the center of his work. He is indeed the
Rebel, in the central Romantic tradition of Rebels, but he is as
far from the Byronic hero as he is from its Prufrockian obverse.
We find comedy, wild, strange, but finally very sane, in the most
unlikely of contexts. One memorable moment occurs in the
following passage from the long narrative forming Part II of
Kaddish: Ginsberg is a student at Columbia visiting his mother
in downtown Manhattan during one of the uneasy periods of
relief from her complete madness:

One time I thought she was trying to make me come lay her—flirting to herself at sink—lay back on huge bed that filled most of the room, dress up round her hips, big slash of hair, scars of operations, pancreas, belly wounds, abortions, appendix, stitching of incisions pulling down in the fat like hideous thick zippers—ragged long lips between her legs—What, even, smell of asshole? I was cold—later revolted a little, not much—seemed perhaps a good idea to try—know the Monster of the Beginning Womb—Perhaps—that way. Would she care? She needs a lover.

The long verse reaches a kind of climax of grotesque horror with the mention of the zippers and the lips: she has become a creature from a horror movie. But with "smell of asshole" he, while seeming to add to the repulsiveness, nevertheless recovers his humanity (beautifully) by remembering hers—it makes her a creature like himself again. Which among us has never had a smelly asshole, after all? And the whole passage turns to his puzzled attempt to think of what it is right to do, his tone of casual sanity so inadequate to the situation, the hilarity to his clumsy tone of kindness ("seemed perhaps a good idea to try"). It restores the sense of proportion.

Humor does not subvert the effects of the entire subversive work, then, but it does subvert any possibility of solemnity. The great final line to his famous early poem "America" is "America I'm putting my queer shoulder to the wheel." I first read that when I disapproved of Ginsberg's poetry a good deal, but even my outraged sense of decorum in the prim 1950s was not proof against the line. However, it is not only disarmingly funny, it is also the whole point: the self who has been making the denunciations of the poem is irregular, individual, subversive—and not even to be classified with other rebels, because he is queer, and people in 1956 didn't admit to being queer. (It just wasn't done.) And later his continued rebellion and protest is clarified and distinguished by the sharpness of his observation, which is as likely to turn in on himself as outward on society or political events: the rebel has become an aging teacher "half-bald, palsied lip." He adheres to the truth of the record, he adheres to the truth of its discrepancies.

In his poetry, then, we find the factual record of the personal life, we find the political record, and we also find the visionary record. Of course all three overlap to some extent, but it is possible to distinguish them. By vision I refer to the supernatural world that Isaiah and Blake, for example, claimed literally to witness. When Blake looks at a thistle,

> With my inward eye 'tis an old Man grey
> With my outward a Thistle across my way.

But Ginsberg does not, I think, make exactly this sort of claim to involuntary vision during the waking life—he does not claim it in his mature poetry, anyway. The main sources of his visions are drugs and dreams, in fact, and his poetry makes a specific and unusual emphasis on such sources. The Moloch section of *Howl* was evoked by the Sir Francis Drake Hotel in San Francisco ("Moloch whose eyes are a thousand blind windows!") seen from Nob Hill after taking peyote. "Wales Visitation" is a record of LSD taken on a Welsh mountainside, where the mists may perhaps be shifting in the wind or may instead be pulsing in his mind: he sees "the satanic thistle that raises its horned symmetry / flowering above sister grass-daisies' pink tiny / bloomlets angelic as lightbulbs." This thistle is different in kind from Blake's, I need hardly point out. But for me most striking are those poems in which the dead return in dreams (as they do to all of us, don't they?), ranging from "Dream Record" of 1955 to "White Shroud" of 1983. In the first of these he converses with Joan, the wife of William Burroughs, who had been killed in a William Tell-like accident a few years before: their dialogue has something of the tranquil sadness we find in some of Dante's interchanges with the dead; in the second he enters a sort of dream retirement with Naomi, dreaming a happier end to that tormented life, in which they share a semi-street existence in a cave opening onto an alleyway. Between these two there are many other poems based on dream work, none of them negligible. There are also poems that *seem* like visions, but may be termed so only as a courtesy title, being probably derived from the regular exercise of the poetic imagination. Such a poem is "Under the world there's a lot of ass, a lot of cunt," in which a terrifying scatological tide flows into the even more terrifying flood of human poisons, chemical weapons, and bits of human bodies that float among them.

With its cumulative and incantatory force, this last poem resembles much of Whitman, being designed as a catalogue—which, though not random, is perhaps the most primitive of poetic structures. For Ginsberg it has always been the preferred structure, though closely followed by that of the narrative. Its potential limitations are obvious: the listed items have to carry the full weight of the reader's interest in turn, without much help from each other, though ideally their sequence should make some sort of gathering sense. In some of Ginsberg's poems, I must admit, neither of these requirements is met; and the result is likely to be tedium. For one of the more unfortunate results of the Ginsbergian honesty is to be found in a kind of literalness of spirit: he is capable of spelling out details at great length like some interminable medieval poet; and he himself is, for better or worse, a diffuse poet.

In this connection, his reaction to Basil Bunting's *Briggflatts* is of great interest. He appears to have read it on its publication in 1965, and immediately admired it, paying it the tribute of imitation, for he wrote a poem about that time, "Studying the Signs," to which there is the subtitle *"After Reading Briggflatts."* To this in turn he appends a note starting: "Late long poem by English master Basil Bunting . . . who'd suggested to Ezra Pound that Poetry be equated with Condensation." (The famous reference may be checked in Chapter 4 of Pound's *ABC of Reading*.) But for all Ginsberg's good will toward them, he does Bunting and Pound a certain injustice: the equation was more than a suggestion, it was a generic description, even an insistence, and Ginsberg's displacement of emphasis becomes a misunderstanding curiously embodied in his imitation, which takes off from certain minor stylistic characteristics of *Briggflatts* while consisting of an unabridged catalogue of *all* the advertising signs in Piccadilly Circus. In the 41 lines there is content sufficient for perhaps one haiku, lines in which Bunting could have packed ten years of autobiography. Bunting also admired Whitman, and from his early years, but he drew from him the strengths he needed, and he remarked on at least one occasion that "the poet's best friend is his waste-paper basket." Ginsberg genuinely misses the point that "condensation" is not a mere grace of style, a rhetorical device, but for Bunting the essence of poetry: in condensed language thought and feeling are so concentrated that precisely *there* is that intensity of effect that the most admired poetry consists of.

Ginsberg on the other hand tries to achieve such intensity by means of accumulation rather than of condensation. Of course he has precedents: just for example, the two wedding poems of Spenser, that most diffuse of poets, the extraordinary beauty of which is dependent on the very long-windedness; and Ginsberg's own diffuseness works often in a slightly similar manner, however different the two poets may seem: by the sheer staying power of his enthusiasm, by the sustained play of his energy. For there is no doubt of the fact that the leisurely process of accumulation may add up to a kind of force unavailable to the poets of succinctness, the force of the large inclusive grasp as opposed to that of the tightly clenched fist.

The principle of his style may well derive from the importance he gives to *erotic* anarchy. The eroticism of the poem "Many Loves" takes the form of a lingering enumeration of acts and perceptions. This stylistic lingering is a visible symbol of that expansive and generous spirit that Ginsberg strives for, so that even anger may become a lingering litany, as in *Howl*, and even lament over anguished recollection may become a lingering narrative, as in *Kaddish*.

What we seldom experience in his poetry, however, is that crystallization of feeling and thought and experience in a single line, or in a few lines, which we find in Blake's Sunflower or Rose poems or in "Song of Myself":

> If you want me again, look for me under your boot soles.

True, he is not incapable of such simultaneous small-scale realization and wide suggestiveness. He does it, for example, in the last line of "America," but he does it seldom. At the opposite extreme we may come against stretches of excessive diffusion, where iteration becomes simply monotony: witness those sections of travelogue entitled "These States," in which tape-recorded details follow one another in relentless accretion, or those comparatively late rhyming poems, in which the demands of the doggerel lead to page after page of extended content.

These are the weaknesses of the *Collected Poems,* but it is as well to remember that most collections of a lifetime's work have their longueurs, and that the kind of poems I here complain about occupy a comparatively small proportion of a long and otherwise lively volume.

As I have suggested, his successes just as much as his failures derive from accumulation of documentation. Where they work best for me, they do so because the sensory detail depends on a narrative, and if I had only an hour to persuade an open-minded reader of Ginsberg's virtues, I would spend it by pointing to four comparatively short narratives, two early and two late: "Aunt Rose" and "Many Loves," "Manhattan May Day Midnight" and "Mugging." Of these "Aunt Rose" is the most familiar, having been reprinted in numerous anthologies. Its power is obvious. Ginsberg throws all his material in—comic, banal, sentimental (though it is all finally subordinated to a dominant mode of pathos), and every emotion is decisively evoked because it rises from a mass of sturdy physical detail. "Now might I *see* you," he says to his dead aunt (the italics are mine), and she comes over to us more distinctly and fully than any other poetic relative I can recall at a time when we have a veritable glut of poetry about family members. Characteristically, Ginsberg sees his childhood self as ludicrously vulnerable, poised naked like an allegory of modesty on the top of the toilet so that his aunt can dab calomine lotion on poison ivy blotches: "I an ignorant girl of family silence," he says of his untried puberty. We remember the odd word "girl" when he uses it again at the end of the poem, this time of the maiden aunt herself, who appears in the oxygen tent as a "blue veined unconscious girl." It has come to signify someone taking no part in full adult experience. In this exquisite poem as in so many of Ginsberg's others, the comic effect is inextricably intertwined with the serious.

"Many Loves" was written two years before this, in 1956,

but did not appear in print until thirty years later, "for reasons of prudence and modesty," Ginsberg explains. It opens with the words, "Neal Cassady was my animal," and we realize almost at once the way we are to take this phrase. "My" does not indicate possession, being used instead as in the phrases "my teacher" or "my hero," for an animal is a being with access to certain kinds of knowledge which a human has to *learn*. The poem could well be prefaced by a quotation from that apparently so different writer, E. M. Forster: I am thinking of the following phrases from *Maurice*, his one novel that doesn't collapse from the weight of its own romanticism or from the self-sabotage of its irony, where he speaks of "the flesh educating the spirit . . . and developing the sluggish heart and the slack mind against their will. . . ." The poem details the first step in such an education, the lesson which acts as incentive to all that follow, in which the flesh instructs the spirit, in which opposites collaborate, in which one's pleasure is also another's, in which self-gratification and giving are one, crudeness and delicacy are one, roughness and gentleness are one. It may be taken, too, as a perfect instance of that Soul-Making Keats spoke of.

The movement and diction of the poem are biblical more than Whitmanian, Lawrentian more than biblical (compare "Snake"):

> And he seeing my fear stretched out his arm, and put it
> around my breast
> Saying "Draw near me" and gathered me in upon him:
> I lay there trembling, and felt his great arm like a king's
> And his breasts, his heart slow thudding against my back,
> and his middle torso, narrow and made of iron, soft at my
> back,
> his fiery firm belly warming me while I trembled.

It is the rhythm and language of reverence, of awe, of sanctity without sanctimoniousness. What ecstasy is in this poem is not the distant idealized ecstasy of the "lark from Heaven, or near it" but the literally experienced ecstasy of the man who wrote it, its stages enumerated and specified. The accretion of incident is essential to the poem, as is its considerable length.

Its combined strength and tenderness make it unique among erotic poems. Whitman and Lawrence never dared write like this; Rochester is by contrast crudely cynical and full of self-hatred—he would not even have grasped what was going on; only Marlowe, perhaps, in *Hero and Leander*, approaches the defiant freshness of enthusiasm and delight found here. There is certainly nothing even approaching it to be found in the multitudinous anthologies of gay poetry that afflict the bookstores nowadays (yes! isn't the twentieth-century section of the *Penguin Book of Homosexual Verse* simply *vapid* and *trivial*?). The reader who doesn't know this poem should look it up at once, and mark especially the eloquent invocation to "the smooth mount of [Cassady's] rock buttocks," in the course of which, as usual, semi-comic elements are readily digested by the overall tone of reverence.

The other two poems, from about twenty years later, are what I consider the best because subtlest political poetry: the politics in them is indirect, but the more persuasive for that. It does not consist of slogans, nor of reference to newspaper events true no doubt but not imaginatively realized; rather it details the images that appear on the screen of the individual consciousness, in the order of their appearance, without evident selection or manipulation—and the whole picture is one of social conditions, toward which the poet's attitude is clearly implied. Again, scale is important to such poetry, since Ginsberg needs adequate space for the accumulation of the images. Both poems take place in the Lower East Side of New York City where he lives. The copious detail is swiftly absorbed, all of it functional and vivid.

"Manhattan May Day Midnight" responds to that feeling we have all had increasingly over the last twenty years that the Empire has begun to get out of hand. There is still immense power at the top, but there is an even more immense decay apparent in the rest of the body: the impulses of Whitman have long since been left behind, and have turned rather to involuntary spasms, signaling the increasing pull of death.

Explicitly this poem is about suppression, the buried, the murdered bodies under floor boards and the rotting gas pipes beneath the streets: the servants of the Empire, seen in terms of their work clothes only, go about their business patching up what they can; Ginsberg watching them wonders about ancient Rome and Ur: "were they like this?" he asks, and again I am reminded of many a moment in Thomas Hardy's poetry.

In "Mugging," "a boy stepped up, put his arm around my neck / tenderly I thought for a moment, squeezed harder, his umbrella handle against my skull." The account is hardly melodramatic: who but Ginsberg would mistake the start of a mugging for an embrace? As usual, he laughs at himself. He is fully aware of the danger, but he never distorts it. He tries to calm the muggers and himself with a ritualized chant "Om Ah Hūm" and when they leave him in an abandoned storefront he rises "thinking Om Ah Hūm didn't stop em enough," opining "the tone of voice too loud"—a disarming Ginsbergian joke against the reassurances and inadequacies of the self.

The second part of "Mugging" is about what happens afterwards. He calls the police from a store, talks with people on the street: if the account is, finally, didactic, it is only subtly and indirectly so—it is a living picture of a run-down New York neighborhood as capitalist sink, an overrun *Blade Runner* human warren in which most individuals are well intentioned but crowded, powerless, and confused: it consists entirely of vigorous instances, Ginsberg's perception of them controlled by that delicate sense of proportion based in his humor. It is all the more persuasive a political poem for not seeming to be one, showing us rather the detail and substance of social conditions on a particular street. He ends

> . . . passing empty apartments, old lady with frayed paper
>   bags
> sitting in the tin-boarded doorframe of a dead house.

She is an enigmatic figure: is she immobilized by her life or is she secretly resourceful, simply catching her breath? There's no way of knowing. That's part of the complicated point that this sophisticated poet is making.

Each of these four poems carries a distinct force of its own. The energy sustained is probably greater than that of any other living poet. Each poem also has its own shapeliness, but we shall not recognize it if we are thinking of Bunting or Marvell, for it is more akin to that of the larger-scale poets like Spenser or Browning. Perhaps we have focused too exclusively on succinctness, since the Imagists, and should have realized that there are other possibilities.

Having read them, the reader might well go back to the beginning of the *Collected Poems* and read right through the book, as I did. It is an *enjoyable* book, informed by a continual honesty of intention and execution, by a constant energy of attack, by humanity of spirit and wild humor, and by aspirations toward ecstasy and vision that may recall to us earlier claims and prerogatives of poetry forgotten in the age of Larkin. It is the record of a career I find more exemplary with each succeeding year.

Surefire Diver

Jack Sharpless

I didn't know Jack Sharpless well, but I often saw him around San Francisco—doing his errands on Haight Street, attending a seminar given by Robert Duncan at the Zen Center, drinking in some bar South of Market, chatting with friends at a street fair, or hurrying off on a bus in his black bow tie to his job as a waiter at the Bohemian Club. You couldn't miss him: he was as tall and thin and handsome as one of his own poems—which seems to gangle down the page in a way that at first looks merely casual but then you come to understand after all that it really makes a figure for which there is no alternative. I don't think I knew that he was a poet until I read of his receiving an important prize from Britain in 1985. He died of AIDS, in his thirties, in 1988.

Like the war in Vietnam, AIDS is the subject of much poetry and is also a killer of poets. Neither the poetry about it nor the poets killed by it are necessarily talented, however, which in a way makes the sadness even greater. But no special pleading is necessary for *Presences of Mind,* which is a sturdy and self-sufficient collection. Sharpless was, evidently, a real professional: never having had a single poem accepted for publication, he continued to plan his inclusive schemes beforehand and to pare down the poems themselves until they were

---

Review of *Presences of Mind: The Collected Books of Jack Sharpless* (Frankfort, Ky.: Gnomon Press, 1989). Reprinted from *Poetry Flash* 203 (February 1990).

an absolute minimum. In his work, nothing goes to waste, every word is necessary.

This attractively produced volume is edited by Ronald Johnson, who has supplied a short but tactful and moving introduction. It is subtitled "The Collected Books" because, it appears, Sharpless wrote his brief narrow poems only as parts of "books" or groups. It is debatable whether they are to be defined as suites or serials or something altogether more loose. Perhaps in fact the association between parts is different with each whole. In the first, "quantum," it seems random enough. "Quantum" consists of twenty-four very short poems printed in capitals "as if carving on stone," in Johnson's phrase. Thus they resemble those inscriptions on stones that the concrete poet Ian Hamilton Finlay places at intervals through his gardens-as-poems in Europe. They are part riddling definitions, part epigrams, as if for the reader to pause at and ponder while wandering through Sharpless's imaginary garden. They are at once teasing and learned, almost like proposals for poems to be completed only in this way, by the reader's response to them.

The spirit of play here in evidence joins with the spirit of learning in the other three books too. For, make no doubt about it, whatever their historical or etymological sources, the poems are always immediately enjoyable, as not all poetry is. "Inroads" is probably the easiest of approach among Sharpless's works, since we all start with some familiarity with the history, or the self-created myth, of Elizabeth I, whose consciousness is speaking in it. It consists of a series of half-hourly moments from the last night of the dying queen, all uttered in the same distinctive voice. The "inroads" of the title may be those that death makes into life—but they may equally well be those that the still-live intelligence makes into the process of dying. The contents range through memories, epigrams, images observed from the deathbed, and the maxims of a monarch. Elizabeth regards her own "lean / & fearful / visage" in a looking-glass, she catches a tabby cat in the act of watching squirrels through a leaded window of the palace, she recalls the head of Essex on a stake, and sees her present household "cold / as a / March / hare's / morning / tracks / in old / snow / at / sun / down." "Inroads" amounts to a new kind of interior monolog and reads like the flashes from another Gerontion—but a dying, plucky, female Gerontion.

The third book is "A Soldier in the Clouds: Variations on a Parish Hymn Recurring in Dreams and Nightmares of Aircraftsman T. E. Shaw." Sharpless now speaks through the voice of another English notable, for this is the name under which T. E. Lawrence enlisted in the British air force and army in trying to escape from his more famous earlier career as Lawrence of Arabia. He took the name from his friend George Bernard Shaw, to whom he once started a letter "Dear Public Shaw" and signed it, accurately, "Yours, Private Shaw." So this is to be a more private assemblage of utterances than the Elizabeth series. His dreams and nightmares, which are about disruption, are endured "in the clouds"— that is, after his death in the motorcycle accident, and they touch not only on the desert war and things of his past, but on the future, on events taking place after his lifetime, the travels of the Windsors in Germany, for example, or the discoveries of loot at Goering's bombed headquarters. The method is the same as with Elizabeth, but taken farther—this group being less literal, less sequential, looser in organization and more daring in scope. The range of material that is permitted into the Aircraftsman's dreams is wider. Sharpless still uses only one or two words to a line (and for the sake of space I have to run them together when quoting); this is a device used many years before by Mina Loy, and has the curious effect of leaving it up to the reader to determine the pace of the verse movement, for it seems to give equal weight to a preposition or conjunction as to a noun or verb. The power of the writing, in any case, is clear: "& / a sea / otter's / handsome / surefire / dives / through / mirrors / of / flesh." Such a passage is dazzling—Sharpless is like Hart Crane for a moment in the way he brings together the animal's action and an action of the imagination. The sea otter's dive is analogous to one taken by the Aircraftsman's mind, or by the poet's, for that matter.

Ronald Johnson tells us, tantalizingly enough, of the book

Sharpless was engaged on at his death: "Working Stiffs," which he describes as the "street raps from a defiant roustabout to a deaf universe," but he quotes only six lines from it. The last book in this collection is entitled "The Fall of the X Dynasty," consisting of sixteen separate poems related to the fall of a hypothetical Chinese dynasty. Several of them deal with isolated characters, a maid, a second-class concubine, a pilgrim. One of the best is "The Tyrant":

> 150,000
> young soldiers'
> sweet bodies
> lined the roads
> to Llasa and
> the outer steppes,
>
> yet he sat
> drinking it up
> with the old boys,
> unembarrassed.

In such lines, a little longer now, Sharpless shows us how a couple of touches of restrained irony can do more than a dozen righteous slogans. "Drinking it up / with the old boys" might seem almost friendly if he didn't elsewhere place the tyrant and his works so precisely, with the words "sweet" and "unembarrassed," triumphs of understated grief and contempt. There is boldness in the attempt to say so much with so little, as there is boldness in the way Sharpless jumps from one image to another at the end of "The Widow":

> Jasmine once again
> incenses
> late summer nights,
>
> though no trace of
> your smoky fragrance
> rekindles these haunts.
>
> Thought I saw
> cities afire
> on the horizon.

The "you" is her dead husband, of course. The relation between the decorous suppressions of language like "haunts" and "incenses" with the heated excitement suggested by the imagery, the movement, and the omitted personal pronoun is surely a small achievement of a high order.

Small, but not so small as all that. *What Maisie Knew* or a short poem by Catullus might seem small to some, after all. Sharpless seems to have appreciated the condensations of the Objectivists, particularly of the less central ones: Johnson mentions Bunting (who said "the poet's best friend is his wastepaper basket"), and I would add Niedecker as well, though Sharpless is more sophisticated than she and, dare I say it, a more substantial poet. It was perhaps from them that he learned the ways in which concision is not merely a negative virtue but the chief creator of tautness and intensity in a poem.

As I have mentioned already, this volume should be a source of much enjoyment to the reader—for its language, so meticulously controlled, so crisp and condensed, for its quickness and intelligence, for its subtlety of feeling, and for the brightly defined instances of its imagination. There is also the wonderful sense of playfulness that is never so private that it bores us by making us feel left out. His lightness and charm make us want to play in his poetry as well, and by reading it we do, we do.

Fever in the Morning

Jim Powell

It seems a lean time for poetry. The New Formalists and the Language Poets compete for our attention, but each group mirrors the other in the incompleteness of its ambitions. The first, complacency at its heart, has no interest in stylistic experiment, and the second scoffs at "subject," placing the term between quotation marks as if referring to some laughable affectation.

Jim Powell's remarkable first book is therefore all the more satisfying in that he avoids both such denials. He is, for one thing, unashamedly concerned with his subject matter, which not only sets him off in the first place but puts the pressure on him to experiment with structure, sentence length, and rhythms in ways that serve to elucidate while rendering more complex.

The first line of his first poem is also the title of the book: "It was fever that made the world," a bold and questionable proposition, thus isolated, that excess is a natural function. Well, it is and it isn't, we may qualify, and in doing so we predict the way the book itself is to explore the implications of this opening. For, having presented it on its own, Powell now proceeds to limit it by the poem it leads into:

> It was fever that made the world
> burn last summer, that afternoon

Review of *It Was Fever That Made the World*, by Jim Powell (Chicago: University of Chicago Press, 1989). Reprinted from *New Republic*, August 13, 1990.

> when I lay watching the sun pour
> its incurable folly slantwise
> into a plum tree's crest,
>
> infusing it till the whole crown glowed
> red as infected blood translucent
> in a syringe.

We are caught at once in the heart of contradictions, however they may be sanctioned by tradition. To call the sun's bounty "incurable folly" classes the heat of procreation with the impulse of the intravenous drug-taker. Powell pursues his imagery of hectic reds through the thirty-five lines of the poem, from blossom and infected blood to the flushed faces of dancers at a rock concert "thriving" on their fever, and finally to

> . . . taillights queueing at the tollbooths
> Friday night, then streaming up the bridge
> till all five lanes of their sharp reds merge
> toward the city's bright towers.

Each image has been linked to the others by an illusion of sequence, the real sequence being in the poet's mind only, and, "merging," they culminate in this suggestion, which is somehow both to the point and beside it. What justifies the reckless joy of the verse movement's final unimpeded sweep? What connects the latent promise of the city's towers with either plum blossom or infected blood? Health and fever are to remain thus mysteriously compromised throughout Powell's book.

The complication and deepening of the central concept in this poem are performed chiefly by the amassing of instances. The sheer variety of what Powell is able to pack in is amazing. Each of his poems is like an enormous club sandwich, the tastes of its ingredients both complementing and rubbing off on one another. It appears that he has learned about sandwiches largely from Horace, two of whose odes he has translated in this volume. In them, the subject is changed about halfway through, making what appears an abrupt new start with the switch from the snowdrifts of a mountain to the summer play of lovers in the city, or from Cleopatra as Rome's sinister opponent, depraved and power-mad, to Cleopatra as clear-eyed heroine. Thus, as Charles Towan Beye says, "The initial stance is perverted, denied, or redefined by the end," and the self-adjusting structure of the poem constitutes a continuing lively example for experiment.

If you add to the second start a third and a fourth, and so on, as Powell does, you end with an inclusive poem indeed, one with room for many different kinds of health and sickness, learning and spontaneity, myth and reminiscence, particularly if your vehicle is the long complex sentence in which subordinate clauses offer ample opportunity for human contrariness to find a means of escape or of further self-entrapment. The final poem of the book consists of a single fifty-line sentence, and the sentence is in fact Powell's primary poetic unit, gathering up material as it goes along, both tentative and assured, in quest of its own end. Did he perhaps learn its potential from that so different poet Robert Duncan?

The same sentence, the same poem, may offer simultaneous accommodation to the ancient Mediterranean or to the Northern California of our own time: Virgil speaking about the nature of unborn souls is set beside an overgrown Oakland yard; the god Pan sodomizing a billy goat shares the expression of a lustful glance intercepted across the room at a party in Berkeley. The classical gods have fully entered Powell's mind, where they lead a wirily conceptual life. But the Bay Area defines the very conditions of his body; the poetry engages it in physical terms, those of a place that the poet has grown up in and lived through detail by detail—far from the familiar journalistic references to hot tubs, etc.

An outmoded gas furnace coming on with a soft explosion in some dark shingled house; "a stuccoed pond / in the half mission style, half moorish entry court / of a store in San Jose" selling lamps; a spot on the hills above Berkeley from which you can watch the lights around the Bay come on at nightfall, house by house, street by street, until they become "a general glow"; and a deer trail tracing its channel of dry, unmitigated heat "through the head-high bristle / of sage buckthorn and manzanita"—such references nourish the poetry with a dense particularity, so that place becomes more than simple background to experience, rather a determinant of it, like Hardy's Wessex or Baudelaire's Paris.

It is never more particularized than in "Revisiting the Haight," where specifics are both sharply themselves and at the same time suggestive of wider contexts without ever turning into mere impoverished emblems. Like most of the other poems, it is written in patterned stanzas made up of accentual lines that are run over as a matter of course, even between stanzas, so that the form is both—in a curious way—elegantly courted and smoothly neglected. A stable pattern and its loss is also the subject explored by the interinvolved and rapidly changing imagery of the poem:

> That year, sea-fog in tufted hanks
> spun through the eucalyptus tops
> below our attic flat,
> thick coiling strands that looked as if
> they passed right through the limbs—intact—

There are at least four times in the speaker's life that are distinguished, four fresh Horatian starts. He is found walking by the house he used to live in, and recalls not only that time twelve years ago but also an earthquake of a month ago and the events of last night. Similarly disparate images are crowded into temporary closeness throughout the poem; pushed together by tremor or random wind, to which he is finally able to turn, seeking shelter not from but in randomness itself. For he and his lover of last night, unlike the sea-fog escaping the branches, continue to "tangle," meet and stay met, so that what may have been random conjunction becomes meaningful.

I would class this as one of the high achievements of the collection, with the opening poem, "Lighting the Furnace," "Song," "The Crooked House," "Between the Teeth," and "Circe." This last starts:

> All the new young men
> have come to crowd around her knees again
> and lean toward her lips,
> sitting bewitched at these feet their grandfathers
> once nuzzled with drugged snouts.

I find it difficult to overpraise the ease of this writing, which in one act combines succinct physical presentation and explanation of it. It is a charming conceit besides, that the original sailors of Odysseus should have given way to a generation of fans who come to sit at the feet of the aged enchantress. But we find at the end a delayed dedication, to Olga Rudge, the mistress of Ezra Pound, and rereading it we realize that the poem is about the witchcraft within sex and poetry: Circe/Olga and Odysseus/Ezra have been indeed a mutual pair, of whom she remains to tell "how he subdued her—as if, remembering, / she possessed him still."

Endeavor in poetry may be like endeavor in love: both entail the entrance into a fever in which health and ill-health are indistinguishable. (Pound's fascism and his greatest poetry have the same source; Circe's power as Muse is identical with her magic that turns men into pigs.) But only by passing through fever may the poem be written—the subduing of the enchantress by which she takes possession of you, and thus both of you are equal in a kind of entwined energy.

It is perhaps here that Jim Powell, not yet forty, most shows his superiority to many of his contemporaries and seniors. He not only understands the way in which opposites are necessary to one another, he achieves his knowledge in the poem, and so we grasp it as we read. In the meeting of opposites—whether of disease and health or of sea-fog and branches or of Circe and Odysseus—he has tapped a subject matter that is endless and important, and by the thoroughgoingness and the subtlety of his exploration shows he has the power to do almost anything.

II

Two Essays on
Robert Duncan

The High Road

A Last Collection

When Elizabeth Bishop and Robert Duncan met in 1969, there was an immediate mutual attraction. They saw a lot of one another that year she lived in San Francisco, both being talkative people with a robust sense of humor and great personal warmth. Hearing Duncan regret that marijuana had never had any effect on him because he didn't know how to inhale, she made a batch of cookies laced with the stuff and made sure it took. Both afterwards described with glee how it reduced him to a mass of giggles on the carpet. The ladylike poet from the East Coast and the wild man of the West Coast were not exactly abiding by their public reputations, it seemed. Of course, they despised those reputations, based as they were on imprecise characterization and partisan reading. But they were baffled by each other's poetry, as they continued to inform their friends. Though they exchanged books, they did not discuss either them or poetic theory.

After all, they had been pursuing their own projects for some time, and the poetics behind the two projects were fundamentally opposed in a way that their personalities were not. Bishop took the low road and Duncan took the high road, you might say, and the low road has proved to be a good deal more popular with readers and critics, though she never lived to

Review of *Ground Work II: In the Dark,* by Robert Duncan (New York: New Directions, 1987). First appeared, in a shortened version, as "Containing Multitudes," *Times Literary Supplement,* December 16–22, 1988.

benefit from the steady sales of her last book and her *Collected Poems*. Her attitude is essentially social, her manner conversational; you notice her charm, her urbane modesty, her *intelligence*. Duncan's attitude is both more private and more public, more oracular perhaps, whether from being experimental or visionary; you react often with admiration, sometimes with perplexity. Yet when he died at the age of sixty-nine, just as *his* last book was published, there were many who considered him the best poet we had. He was master of a twentieth-century grand style—but more, he was admired for the range of the risks he took: so Robert Creeley described him as his "hero of possibility," and John Montague had spoken of him as "the greatest living example of the full modern enterprise in poetry, an unashamed response to the living muse of Language." Perhaps by unashamed he meant that Duncan disregarded just that literary decorum by which Bishop abided so admirably.

You do not have to choose between Bishop and Duncan any more than you have to choose between William Blake and Samuel Johnson; but if some have, and have chosen to reject the achievement of Duncan, it is because they have found it disconcerting and alarming. He left behind him a large body of work, poetry and prose, much of it in print in the United States but much uncollected, which will all eventually be brought together in seven large volumes from the University of California Press. His writing may be found disconcerting in that very exploration of possibility Creeley mentioned: for there was a strong element of the unpredictable in Duncan— he was a daredevil rather as a cat is, jumping down into wells of obscurity or on to formidable spiked fences where no reasonable creature would have ventured. Moreover his ideas and practice, from the start, called into question the assumptions about style that dominated when he began to write in the 1940s and 1950s. In one of the essays collected in *Fictive Certainties* (1985) he says provocatively, "I like rigor and even clarity as a quality of a work—that is, as I like muddle and floaty vagaries. It is the intensity of the conception that moves me." Not just toleration but *liking* for muddle would have been more than a little alarming to those educated on Brooks and Warren's *Understanding Poetry*, though current critical assumptions now would be more hospitable to such a statement.

Yet Montague is correct in referring to "the full modern enterprise," for if the New Critics had their reading of it, then Duncan had his, which was more expansive. On reading Browning in his teens, he had decided to be a poet, and from Browning to Pound had been an easy transition: his primary allegiance from that time on was certainly to Modernism, but it was not a Modernism at all like that of his contemporaries, it was a different mix. He was proud to proclaim himself a "derivative" poet, refusing to see the word as pejorative. We all derive, of course, we choose our own tradition, we have our influences—though it is as well to note, with Michael André Bernstein, that Duncan's influences are not of the *fathers* but rather of *allies*. He finds his allies up and down history (Dante is one, Rumi another), but what makes him unusual is the makeup of his particular home-circle of influences, which are picked equally from the Modernists and from the Romantics, so that Blake and Shelley and Whitman are found sitting around the same table as Pound and Stein and H.D. Duncan noticed the continuity between Modernist and Romantic long before most of the critics did: the specific life of his home-circle came from his connecting the Romantic admiration for impulse with the theory of "open form" that he, following Charles Olson, found suggested by the practice of Pound and the later W. C. Williams.

Not only Pound and Williams, perhaps. We can see it foreshadowed even in Yeats, even in such a familiar poem as "In Memory of Major Robert Gregory," where the interruption of the poem's proposed structure becomes the poem's actual structure; but Yeats's apparent submission to impulse is, characteristically, a calculated dramatic effect rather than a decision spontaneously made during the writing—the care and cunning of the style, its very finish, serving to place all impulsive decision many drafts anterior to the version we read. Nevertheless, the poem may be taken as a link in the long chain reaching from the associationism of the early Romantics like Coleridge to Olson's theory and practice of what he called projective verse and Duncan called open form, a theory which Duncan praises in the accents of the willful Romantic as "proposing a primordial, titanic, unaccountable spirit in poetry, beyond measure," and for which he aptly finds a source and antecedent in Emerson on Spontaneity.

The poem written in open form is meant to be viewed less as an artifact than as part of a *process* (a word Duncan uses repeatedly in his criticism), which may take directions unanticipated in the original conception, depending on accident more than on predetermined design. If an ant or a wasp comes into Pound's cage in the Pisan detention camp, then it also comes into the poetry Pound is writing at that time. To some extent, of course, the incorporation of chance during the act of composition has been the practice of all poets, but the "unaccountable spirit" of open form, emphasizing the unforeseen, concludes by making for a radically different kind of poetry. Pound refers to "Brother Wasp" and then remembers that the word for wasp in Italian is feminine: so, "la vespa, *la* vespa" he corrects himself—but he does not strike out his "mistake," *he incorporates both mistake and correction,* thus defining a poetry of spontaneity as he writes. Duncan goes even farther: a true Freudian, he believes in the centrality of what we call accident or chance. By our inadvertence and error we find out what we really mean, beyond and beneath purpose. (Such is the gist of his magnificent long essay "The Truth and Life of Myth," which opens *Fictive Certainties*.) Speaking as the Whitmanian poet, he says:

> Walk with me and you will begin to feel who I truly am, even as I find who I truly am as I come into my step fully; indeed, come into your stride with mine and you will begin to find yourself. ("The Adventure of Whitman's Line")

In practice, writing poetry like this, being an exploration directed primarily by the opportunities of the moment, should be subject to neither a fixed purpose before the composition is started nor revision once it is concluded. Everything depends on the energy of the present. Even a misspelling may be a

132

legitimate part of the resulting poem: thus in line 6 of Duncan's "Styx" (*Ground Work II*) the word "woundrous" occurs, describing the paths that water carves through rocks—wondrous wounds in fact. The neologism is just as likely to be a misspelling preserved as a conscious intention embodied, and its suggestions are not therefore less integral to the poem.

The dangers of such a theory to an untalented poet are obvious, and hardly need to be enumerated, since we do not, in any case, seek out the poetry of the untalented. One does, however, train oneself into a talent, training may entail the correction of weak writing, and it is difficult to see how allowance is made for such correction; but perhaps it is permissible not to pursue my reservation at this moment since I am here speaking of a poet already mature. For him the richnesses of possibility are great, so long as he has a vigorous mind and makes himself expert at judging when his imaginative powers are at their highest. It is of course a matter of writing only when you are at your best, and it is also a matter of learning to *be* at your best. But then it is anyway.

Duncan's procedure may be followed most easily in a short poem called "Childhood's Retreat" (*Ground Work*). He starts with a simple proposition, so simple as to be almost trite, but in the fourth line he embarks on a new sentence which is to carry him through all the rest of the poem, in which he enters the verbal means, the suggestions and puns and contradictions, through which "childhood's retreat"—tree-climbing— may be described as no retreat at all, but rather the opposite, a risk in the act of being taken. He remembers the "shaking uncertainties" of the boughs:

> all voices and scenes come back
>
> —the barking of a dog,   autumnal burnings,
> far calls,   close calls—   the boy I was
> calls out to me
> here the man where I am   "Look!
>
> I've been where you
>
> most fear to be."

On this small scale he explores the childhood exploration, his means of doing it granted by the nonce associations of the word "calls." As with his act of composition, his retreat into what seemed a private world of the imagination is actually an advance into a perilous uncharted outer world.

Here it is necessary to recall his book of 1960, *The Opening of the Field*, not only because it remains the most accessible point of entry into Duncan's terrain, but because it is the true start of the project that was to occupy him for the rest of his life. It seems to me, besides, one of the essential books for understanding the history of poetry in English over the last half-century, alongside *Lord Weary's Castle, Briggflatts, Ariel,* etc., not only for its inherent virtues but for the historical reasons I have implied—it embodies the one really influential new theory of poetry advanced in our lifetime.

It is conceived and written *as a book,* each poem linked to many of the others, elaborating on previous themes while proposing new ones. They are connected like "lamps strung among / shadowy foliage." The foliage grows in the "field" of the title, which is conceived of as a field of energy, of activity, of the imagination. It is not a *road*, as a narrative or argument may be considered; still less is it a *series of rooms*, or suite of stanzas. The image of the field is to be taken both in an abstract and in a physical, or pastoral, sense, then: a meadow, a pleasure ground, a pasture, the marsh covering the ruins of Sodom, or the middenheap that promotes fertility, it is all these and more in relationship. Tight-knit correspondences are found not only in the mastering image of the field but also in the detail of its contents: thus, to take one example, the ant from the tale of Cupid and Psyche, referred to in one poem, is related to the ant of the *Pisan Cantos,* referred to in another. The field is full of such correspondences, which are called "rimes," for this is the book in which Duncan initiates one of his open-ended series of poems, "The Structure of Rime," which is to run through all the subsequent books:

The structure of rime is in the rigorous trees repeated that take on the swirl visible of the coast winds and the outcroppings, the upraised and bared granites that define sentences of force and instrument. ("The Structure of Rime XIII")

In the tight involvement of this mesh that is yet open to numberless new strands, even opposites are related, as rot is related to vegetable growth, or as, in a more complex way, Christ is related to Satan. (Duncan cited a Gnostic belief that when Christ looked over the edge of heaven he saw his own reflection far beneath. Like Narcissus he fell in love with it: it was Satan.) His poetic allows for the inclusion of contradictions in the same way that his existence must be acknowledged to contain light and dark, good and evil, peace and war. Thus, though he may be partisan, though he may oppose the Vietnam War, for example, he also has to admit the fact that war, the hatred and violence that it holds, cannot be smugly located outside of himself, but must be recognized as a permanent part of his own imagination and secret desires. One of the themes most emphasized in his poetry, then, is that of "the deeper unsatisfied war beneath / and behind the declared war" ("Achilles' Song," *Ground Work*).

The recognition of an unresolvable internal conflict has important consequences in his poetic. For in the same way that he sees his moral certainties compromised, he wishes to compromise, as he says, his own line of poetry. He even tells us in "The Self in Postmodern Poetry,"

What I would point out in my work as one of its underlying currents is the weaving of a figure unweaving, an art of unsaying what it says, of saying what it would not say. I want to catch myself out.

It is this current that accounts for the most exciting, and the most exasperating, of Duncan's writing: for he trusts his spontaneity so completely that he encourages it to *trip up* his conscious intentions.

Yet there is room for both those intentions and the tripping up within the larger project, which started in the book of 1960 and was continued through *Roots and Branches* (1964), *Bending the Bow* (1968), *Ground Work: Before the War* (1984), and the book under review, *Ground Work II: In the Dark* (1988). The project might be characterized as an attempt to explore the entire field of a spontaneous imagination, which might in turn be characterized in terms of the latest description of the universe—finite but unbounded. His ambition, in fact, is fully as great as Whitman's or Pound's, with *their* finite but unbounded subjects ("these States," "knowledge"): he too wants to include everything he can in the great single poem of his collected work. The risk of inclusiveness is inflation, as I once heard him remark in an aside during a lecture. And he accepted that risk: certainly some of the poetry is inflated, as it is in Whitman and in Pound too, quite simply because, though you may want to include everything in your poem, you cannot write with equal force about everything (unless you are Dante or Shakespeare). But the attempt is heroic, and for all that is inflated or occulted there still remains a large amount of poetry that is fully rewarding and that would not exist without the foolhardy heroism.

Before specifying the rewards of his last book, let me insert a biographical note. In 1972 he announced that he did not intend to issue another collection of his work until fifteen years had passed since *Bending the Bow*. There were no doubt several reasons for his decision, but the comprehensive one was that publication was a form of closure, and he wanted to postpone it so as to leave open for a while the working of his field's ground as a continuous operation not divided arbitrarily into the segments of separate volumes.

The fifteen years stretched into sixteen, and in February, 1984, he suffered a complete kidney collapse. After this date he composed only one two-page poem, an eerie account of his illness, and lived his last four years essentially as a posthumous poet, still talking volubly and on occasion brilliantly (as testified by published interviews), but unable to concentrate long enough to read anything more demanding than the short stories of Kipling and the *Oz* books (he who had devoured books, as he once said, "gluttonously"), let alone write either poetry or prose. Later that year he published *Ground*

Work: Before the War, which as one of his most accurate commentators, Ken Irby, has noted, consists of poetry 1968–1975. The succeeding collection, *Ground Work II: In the Dark,* therefore consists of poems written 1976–1984 and, since two of those years were unexpectedly barren, is probably only half as long as he had hoped it would be.

One reviewer, Tom Clark, has said "it's indeed hard *not* to read this book as a journal of holy dying," but Duncan did not know he was dying until he wrote the last poem, "After a Long Illness." Nevertheless, his health must have been secretly deteriorating during the years of composition, and there is far more about the subjects of death and disease in this collection than in any of the others. It is not for nothing that its subtitle is *In the Dark,* for a major theme is the interpenetration of life and death.

Though the book lacks the cumulative power of *The Opening of the Field* and the bulk of the first *Ground Work,* I find in it that wide range of approach and tone that I have come to expect from him, where improviser and virtuoso meet. If I cannot claim to have completely grasped all that is here, that is a matter for time and patience. I have learned to trust Duncan for what he has given me in the past, as I have learned to trust certain other difficult poets I admire. I shall never elucidate everything, but I understand more with every reading. In any case, there are both serial groups and individual poems here which I can already see as counting among his best. Reading and rereading outward from them, I shall come into possession of more poetry each time I take this book up.

Such a serial group, "An Alternate Life," makes a fitting opening to the collection, for it exemplifies the peculiarities and strengths of Duncan in all their mutual involvement. Here we may appreciate the full adventure of entering the process of a Duncan composition, fifteen pages of it, energetic yet tentative, assertive yet self-revising, opportunistic yet receptive, taking place as it does in some area between directionless flux and rigid authorial control, an area which the poet defines as he goes along. It is about his having fallen in love during a visit to Australia and deals with his return to his household in San Francisco and his lover of many years. We may mark the fact that "household" is a word always associated in Duncan's work with his firmest values: it is not quite the same as "marriage," suggesting rather something "homemade," something built up bit by bit between the foundations and roof-beams of the physical house, individual, specific, improvised. These last three terms also apply to the whole work: Duncan follows the unpredictable currents of feeling, avoiding no awkwardness or inconsistency to make them seem smoother. He sees himself as ridiculous at one point ("An old man's hand fumbles at the young man's crotch"), but he passes no judgment on the two others involved. And the poet of open form is also open in the sense of being frank—if this is about a form of adultery, it is not found with that hypocrisy which is adultery's customary companion.

Hypocrisy would give shape and order to this implied story of adultery; alibis, after all, tend to have classical and tightly knit plots. It is precisely the lack of such a plot that makes the work's overall structure obscure on early readings: nothing is closed off, nothing gets decided; there are no renunciations as there are no condemnations. We are forced to concentrate on the word-by-word realization that is the poem; and the title tells us all we need to know about its general shape: Duncan moves, either physically or emotionally, between alternates, alternate *you*s, alternate *he*s, alternate hemispheres, alternate lives, alternate seasons. On the third page he says, "In the alternate life I am visiting early Spring again," literally the Australian spring, and figuratively everything that spring traditionally suggests. His problem, of course, is in fitting enough contents for two lives into "the one life I am leading." The situation is desperately commonplace, and one of its most commonplace features is that the influence is greatest of whatever place he is currently in: "O daily actual life," he says back home, "I am // deep in your thrall."

Commonplace language for a commonplace situation, the reader might remark of that last phrase. Duncan would say so too. "Deep in your thrall" exemplifies the kind of risk he is prepared to take, with language as with structure; it is

ushly Romantic, certainly timeworn, if only from its endurance at least through the nineteenth century into the movies
and songs of our own. Duncan both *means* it and is aware of
its timewornness, aware that the emotion giving rise to it is
both nineteenth century Romantic and twentieth century
Hollywood—its particular nature tutored as much by Garbo's Anna as by Tolstoy's. I insist on his disconcerting awareness, which is heightened by the variety of other modes of
speech here, one of which is the self-scrutinizing language of
wit, the cool perception of paradox. When "news comes
from the South," he sees it as "gifts from another time I /
most hold in losing." The letter from Australia in his hand,
he holds that other life "in" losing it, that is, both *while* and *by*
losing it. He almost relishes the neatness of the paradox, his
tone is so far outside the conscious self-indulgence of the
earlier phrase. The work is made up of alternating tones and
feelings, then, copresent like so much else here in all their
unbalancing and disturbing possibilities.

The "hero of possibility" necessarily takes such things as his
subject matter, but this is a book written "in the dark," and so
we come to the magnificently eloquent poem "Styx," and the
river where the apparently endless mingling streams of human possibility fall into stasis. "Styx" is organized as description; but every physical detail in it speaks to the death which
will close off this collection:

> And a tenth part of bright clear Okeanos
>   his circulations—mists, rains, sheets, sheathes—
>   lies in poisonous depths, the black water.

"Circulations" is another loaded word for Duncan. It is in
circulation that not only Ocean but blood and song remain
vital: and the water of Styx is the *un*circulating stillness that we
originate from and also "thirst for" (as the last line tells us) "in
dreams we dread." Once more the undeclared war, in which
we thirst and dread at the same time, is brilliantly evoked, and
with the later poem "In Blood's Domaine" he openly enters
the conflict once more.

"In Blood's Domaine" starts by naming "the Angel Syphilis

in the circle of Signators"—and other deadly angels are to follow, Cancer, Tuberculosis, Leukemia. Perhaps the word Signators recalls Pound's "Regents" of Canto LI (and sure enough Duncan seems to be confirming that allusion by, after Pound, introducing the monster Geryon farther on in the poem): like the Regents, the Signators are emblematic functionaries self-appointed to act as a check on human thriving. The difference is that Pound's figures stand for evil, being the Regents of Usury, but Duncan's Signators are beyond good and evil—the spirochetes of syphilis may be seen as embodiments of a life as justified, as daring, and as divine as that of the sparrows pecking on the rhinoceros or of the human beings perched on the globe. They are "attendants of lives raging within life." Is the word Signators then in some way a reference to the DNA code—a suggestion that the signatures of disease are joined with our own so that their lives are transmitted with ours, inextricably "attendant" on all of us?

I should point out that Duncan is not being sentimental or fanciful, the ultimate humanitarian standing up for the rights of syphilitic spirochetes, but is simply affirming the rather traditional belief that the destructive impulse, the pursuit of death, the will to war must all be acknowledged as necessary balance to what we see as the positive and productive tendencies of life, which are in fact defined by the presence of such counter-tendencies. Perhaps it is the intervention of Freud that takes him so far from the late-Romantic optimism of Emerson. "Link by link I can disown no link of this chain from my conscience," he says in recognizing even the Hitler within himself, and through such language looking forward to those other chains in the yet unwritten poem, the last of the book, in which he describes his kidneys as "cloggd with light chains." He is terrified, he is dismayed, even as he contemplates the grandeur of the Angels. He cannot help but acknowledge their strength and their enduring presence within their opposites: "Hel shines in the very word *Health* // as *Ill* in the Divine Will shines."

It is worth pausing over the style of this last line. "Hel" (like "thot" for "thought" and other words elsewhere) suggests Miltonic spelling. This, the capital initials, the inverted word order, and the exalted language all point to a prophetic mode which, in its loftiness and assurance of tone, is not common among the poets we take seriously in the second half of the twentieth century. Such a mode is not invariable in his mature books (there is in fact a most flexibly maintained range of tones throughout this one alone), but it constantly recurs: and much of Duncan's unusualness for a new reader comes from his unfamilar readiness to take what I have called the high road. Historically it has become less used only recently, since poets started to move away from the grand style. Most of us have in recent years taken a very low road indeed, finding our virtues in understatement and our safety in irony; we are tentative and evasive; we disown passion or we clothe it in indirection. Duncan by contrast makes claims for the importance of poetry that are both Poundian and Shelleyan (perhaps Dantean as well): in doing so he holds himself responsible for deep feeling, whether public or personal, without the qualification of irony, and adopts the voice of the seer or the bard even to the extent of giving an archaic cast to his speech. (Before automatically condemning the poetic device of archaism, we would be well advised to remind ourselves that it has a long and respectable history, and was not merely a regrettable Victorian invention.)

It is time to suggest, then, that we pay more attention to the work of a man whose aims and accomplishments have been larger than those of the run of contemporary poets, though assuredly the kind of ambition implied is not stylish on either side of the Atlantic. Ken Irby said in his fine succinct review of the first *Ground Work* in *Conjunctions: 7* (1985): "I take my occasion here as calling for *notice* of the work, not exegesis; that in time." It is still necessary, after Duncan's death, to call for notice. Duncan himself believed abidingly in inclusiveness, and thus disliked the practice of selection and anthology. But such practices have their uses, and when my purpose is to get a neglected poet read more widely, as it is now, one way to go about it is to start naming some of the best poems, in Poundian or Wintersian fashion. Here are some poems which readers interested in poetry might try making their own— they are worth the trouble: "Often I Am Permitted to Return to a Meadow," "This Place Rumord to Have Been Sodom," and "A Poem Beginning with a Line by Pindar" from *The Opening of the Field;* "My Mother Would Be a Falconress" from *Bending the Bow;* "Achilles' Song," "Interrupted Forms," and "A Little Language" (Dante Etudes) from the first *Ground Work;* and from the book under review the poems I have named earlier, as well as "Cherubim (I)" and "After a Long Illness." Having digested these, readers might then care to go on to whole books. They will find they have discovered a poet who alters their idea of the way it is possible to write in their lifetime.

Adventurous Song

Robert Duncan as Romantic Modernist

1

Robert Duncan was proud to call himself a derivative poet. We are all, of course, derivative, but most of us try to cover up our debts when we are aware of them, and to present our work as self-sufficient and self-originating. We are warned by the example of the already mature Theodore Roethke, who acknowledged "I take this cadence from a man named Yeats," but took it without adding enough of his own, so that his later poetry is merely a secondhand Yeats. Duncan too fed on those he admired, but like a true cannibal he digested their virtues to make them his, and they rose in him with a fresh life, both recognizable and altered.

The poet who influenced him most—that is, most strongly and most lastingly—was Pound. But Pound with a difference: Pound as meat from which Duncan drew what nourishment he needed, and even that was modified by all the other poets Duncan made part of his diet. This may not be my Pound or yours, not even Olson's or Bunting's, and it is a mark of Pound's greatness that his poetry has been the source of such various strength.

"I was eighteen in 1937 when I first opened *A Draft of XXX Cantos* . . . [and] set out with Ezra Pound as a master upon the adventure of a poetics to come that is not done with," Duncan

Reprinted from *PN Review* 78 (1991) and from *Threepenny Review* 47 (1991).

recalled, writing for *Agenda* on Pound's eightieth birthday.[1] In 1947 he hitchhiked across the country to visit the master at St. Elizabeths. Dorothy Pound was hospitable, putting him up in the room of her absent son Omar, but she slightly unnerved him. "I cannot understand why Ezra still speaks well of that homosexual, Cocteau," she said to him by the way. ("There I was, not only her guest but sleeping in her son's bed," said Duncan many years later. "My ears must have turned red.") And the last mark of her considerable generosity was to send him on his way with some pamphlets of what he called "hair-raising anti-Semitism." The Pounds, after all, had met in the Edwardian London of "Saki," Kipling, and the elderly James, in which Jews and homosexuals were acceptable only if they were at the same time reticent and rich. But during Duncan's conversation with Pound himself, he found a difference of opinion that he would not have predicted.

> I said: What do you do when statements have the character of a pun in which they go both ways? [Pound] would not allow that a single event or a single statement could be duplicit.[2]

Duncan and the Duplicit Style

The interchange thus summarized is of great interest for what it tells us about both poets. It may be, indeed, that Pound was the more emphatic because of his reaction to Duncan's early poetry, which he had read without enthusiasm, and which showed at that time more of the influence of George Barker, Edith Sitwell, and Hopkins (a standard period mix of the 1940s) than of anyone Pound admired, let alone of Pound himself. The achievement of Duncan's career was to pull himself out of such muddy places into the firmer heights of *The Opening of the Field*. But "duplicity" was as important to the effect of the most fully achieved later poems as it was to the gaudy early ones.

In "Heavenly City, Earthly City," which he had sent Pound before his visit of 1947, there is a conflict between "my Redeemer" and "my Beloved," since Duncan seems unsure if he loves a St.-John-of-the-Cross Jesus or an earthly lover, and the authorial confusion is a gladly accepted part of the poem's subject matter. (Dorothy, if she read it, must have considered the poem pretty reprehensible, so it's possible that her own hair had been raised a bit and her remark about Cocteau was not so casual, after all.) In any case, to Duncan, who had learned not only from Pound but from *Finnegans Wake* and Freud's psychology of errors (for neither of which Pound had any time), all self-confusions, mistakes, and chances offered imaginative opportunities which should not be turned down. Bridges had advised the young Pound to avoid homophones; Duncan, however, came to see them not as distractions from meaning but as clues that lead into deeper meaning. In "A Poem Slow Beginning" of the late 1950s, he was to say, recalling his early years as a student at Berkeley:

> There first I knew
> the companions name themselves
>   and move
> in time of naming upward
>   toward outward
> forms of desire and enlightenment,
>
> but intoxicated
>   only by longing
> belonging to that first company
> of named stars that in heaven
> call attention to a tension
>   in design,
>
>   compel
> as the letters by which we spell words compel
>   magic refinements . . .

Duncan, in fact, is not one of the Mr. Facing-Both-Ways of poetry who lazily think it is somehow artistic to exploit any chance association for the mere whimsical unprosiness of it: he *means* the duplicity. In an idealized Arcadian past, the student-poets rise through acts of self-definition into "outward / forms" of Love and Poetry; and the chances of English spelling teach them esoteric truths: "by longing" we may certainly be led to "belonging," and by our "attention" to an awareness of "a tension." The doubleness that Duncan sought was in an active ongoing embrace between contrary meanings, and he rejoices to find two different senses entwined in a single set of noises, like the human and divine confused in a single lover.

Pound and the Style of Blur

Pound, as we all know, had his own disparate beginnings: those of the young man passionate with learning who interpreted the Spirit of Romance in Rossetti-like terms. "Canzon: Of Incense" shows it at its best. I quote the first stanza, though no extract can demonstrate Pound's skill with this difficult form, in which rhyming from stanza to stanza (but not within the stanza) necessitates a relatively swift verse movement or the pattern will be lost. The writing is remarkable for conveying a heavy languor of feeling through such movement:

> Thy gracious ways,
>> O Lady of my heart, have
> O'er all my thought their golden glamour cast;
> As amber torch-flames, where strange men-at-arms
> Tread softly 'neath the damask shield of night,
> Rise from the flowing steel in part reflected,
> So on my mailed thought that with thee goeth,
> Though dark the way, a golden glamour falleth.
>> (*Collected Early Poems of Ezra Pound*)

It may be a dated theatrical production, but it is a beautiful and accomplished one, with great finish, and deserves the same kind of attention which we give to the early Tennyson (for example the Mariana poems). It is all antique atmosphere, golden and amber. The trouble with it is that it deals with the effect of the Lady rather than with the Lady herself, in a way that we might almost consider late-Jamesian if the idiom were not so different from that of James. The exquisite detail of the effect replaces any possible precision in *her* representation—we have to take her actual behavior and appearance on trust, the source of all this analogy, in such language as "gracious ways" and "glamour." All that we know about her is in the value he places on her. She herself is a blur at the center of the poem—as she is meant to be. But the result is entirely distinct from what Duncan was talking about at St. Elizabeths, for though blur and "duplicity" may both produce ambiguities, the ambiguities are of different sorts. Blurred writing implies bewilderment on the part of the writer, duplicit a knowing ingenuity. And what is more, the Canzon aims for a unity of effect in complete contrast to the restlessness of the passage quoted from Duncan above.

With the intervention of Imagist discipline, Pound is no longer interested in the effect of blur. Setting aside the tonal riddles of *Mauberley* and *Propertius* as constituting a special case, an avenue of ironies entered for a short while but not thereafter explored, we may say that the mature Pound's poetry is astonishingly straightforward, whether in image or in statement or in both: it appeals almost always to hard actuality, to the perception of a defined edge. (Thus Donald Davie subtitled his first study of Pound "Poet as Sculptor.") "As a lone ant from a broken ant-hill / from the wreckage of Europe, ego scriptor" has the same classical hardness, the same unblurred and unriddling definition, as the "Alba" of 1913:

> As cool as the pale wet leaves
> > of lily-of-the-valley
> She lay beside me in the dawn.

(She is a creature of cool flesh and not of "gracious ways.") Primary sense is clearly distinguished from secondary suggestions, as it is too in the line R. P. Blackmur was so taken by: "in the gloom, the gold gathers the light against it." Blur might be called the partial *subject* of that line, but it is not the method, causing us to reflect once again that though stylistic mimesis may be a common and useful effect, its antithesis, the contrast between style and subject, may achieve quite as much. The language here is so compressed and active (even the preposition is charged with meaning) that it goes beyond the merely visual. It is absolutely specific: if I agree with Blackmur that the gloom is also that of time, and add that the gold is what survives, while the light is of understanding (or perhaps value), I do not mean that the line is therefore an allegory merely that it is deeply and richly suggestive: for such abstractions are as embedded in the image as the visual is. And here is where I have to disagree with Blackmur, though he was ahead of his time in discussing Pound at all—for the strength of the line is not, as he claims, just stylistic, but in the whole weight of experience that it carries and sums up. Nor, for all its richness of connotation, is it anywhere ambiguous in my two senses of blurred or duplicit.

Romantic Aspects of the Mature Pound

By 1947, Pound had for long considered himself a didactic writer, in the largest sense. Bunting once remarked: "To illustrate, comment, contrast, organise, the Good Life is presumably the object of the poem [the *Cantos*], as of Dante's."[3] Perhaps the didactic poet thinks he must speak directly or he will defeat his purpose, and in his reported insistence that poetry should have a single meaning Pound sounds as rationalistic as Ben Jonson or Samuel Johnson.

In practice he wasn't, of course, nor were they. And Duncan had already in his own mind claimed Pound as an entirely different writer. What he most valued in him, he said in *Agenda,* was "the sublime and the ecstatic," and an indication of Pound's inclusive genius is that such elements are certainly present in the *Cantos* beside the rational and instructive ones.

Moreover, Duncan had evidently noticed Pound's enduring Romantic connections behind the Confucian and monetary and fascistic didacticisms. Though I have noted the primacy of a single sense in the mature Pound, his poetry is still closer to that of Keats and Rossetti than to that of Catullus or even Pope. I spoke of a classical hardness, but there is also a post-Romantic dependence on the possibilities of connotation that makes his best writing anything but austere: though he keeps the connotations firmly subordinate, he still makes the most of them in their subordination, so that we are left with the senses uncluttered but fully satisfied.

And then there is, even more to the point, Pound's method

of fragmentation, juxtaposition, and collage, which it is surely accurate to see (with Yvor Winters) as the ultimate product of Romantic associationism.[4] By 1991 we have become so accustomed to the accepted interpretation of, say, Canto LI, that we overlook the room for ambiguity, for simple misreading that its method allows. What *is* the connection between usury and the construction of artificial fishing lures, after all? Some of my students coming to this Canto, alert and intelligent but unaware of the by now orthodox interpretations, have made some ingenious connections that would no doubt have distressed the poetry's author. (For example, we might take the very *artificiality* of the lures as the product of a society corrupted by usury.) In fact, though Pound thought his structural method clear, Duncan would have had some justification for considering it duplicit even when the language and imagery admit of no secondary sense.

The Two Uses of *Sordello*

Pound had developed it, in public view as it were, from Browning's in *Sordello;* and when in the late 1970s Duncan gave a seminar—actually a series of monologs or lectures—on Modern Poetry, he chose to start by discussing Browning before going on to Pound and his contemporaries. In the event, he got stuck in the "chokeweed" of *Sordello.*

In Book the First, Browning speaks of

> a certain chokeweed grown
> Since o'er the waters, twine and tangle thrown
> Too thick, too fast accumulating round,
> Too sure to over-riot and confound
> Ere long each brilliant islet with itself . . .
>
> (*Sordello*, 215–19)

"In the extended metaphor here, the Ghibellins are associated with rocks and cliffs, the Guelfs with chokeweed,"[5] says John Pettigrew in a note to a passage which is far longer than what I have just quoted, a passage moreover slammed beside a piece of narrative without any connecting words at all—the transition (if it can be called that) occurring in mid-sentence. From it, you may clearly see how Browning's method leads to that of Canto LI. Item is set beside apparently unrelated item, and it is up to the reader to make a connection (unless a scholar does it for you). Ronald Bush speaks of "*Sordello*'s infamously confusing use of parataxis. For Browning, in order to be authentically modern, a poem must forego narrative continuity and render the fragmentation of a modern consciousness."[6] Between *Sordello*'s parataxis and the full-blown Poundian technique is not far, and you may trace it, as Bush does with accuracy and subtlety, through the three "Ur Cantos."

However, Duncan never reached the twentieth century in his seminar. With much delight he treated the chokeweed as an analogy for Browning's whole complicated involvement with his subject, the long sentences that suddenly change direction in the middle and develop new ramifications. Duncan was able to say to us: "The adventure I propose is, *what do we find in the chokeweed?*" *He* took Browning's poetry as the precursor of an open poetry in which the process of writing gets excitingly out of control, thus admitting interesting accidents and unforeseen directions.

Duncan's Definition of Romanticism

Whereas Pound looked to *Sordello* for a model and found structural possibilities there, Duncan looked to it for a precedent and found anarchic possibilities. We are helped in this way to understand more exactly what Duncan means when he calls himself a poet belonging "in the Romantic vein." In seeking to avoid the rationalistic precisions he distrusted, Duncan probably conflates the ambiguity of blur with the ambiguity of the duplicit statement: in any case, he uses both, as I hope to show, and such distinctions are made irrelevant for the time being by his definition of the Romantic movement as "the intellectual adventure of not knowing."[7]

This formulation, both bold and illuminating, clarifies not only Duncan's view of what he was up to but something of what the Romantic poets themselves had been up to. Its application to even the most obvious of Romantic anthology pieces is at once apparent. Thus Shelley's West Wind, thus negative capability, thus the late-Romantic Yeats's approving use of the word "ignorant," and thus the strange thought of well-read poets condemning books as collections of barren leaves. And though "I cannot see what flowers are at my feet," I plunge into the "embalméd darkness" with all the greater enthusiasm. Embalméd: its perfume is that of plants at the height of their vitality, but it is also that of long-dead corpses, of mummies. The experience plunged into, "not knowing"-ly, is in fact challenging because of its very duplicity. The Romantic poet is for Duncan comparable to the hero of a folk tale who starts off in the face of riddles, ambiguous portents, and the promise of impossible tasks—but the hero starts out on his journey anyway.

> Today I still love, even foolishly, the signs and wonders, felt presences or nearnesses of meaning, where we must follow, in trust, having no more sure a guarantee of our arrival than does the adventurer in a fairy or hero tale.[8]

But by now the reader must feel that it is high time to pay attention to Duncan's almost obsessive reiteration of the word "adventure."

2

Probably the single most common metaphor used in this century for literary activity has been that of exploration. We say the poet or novelist *explores* his subject matter—whether what he explores is experience, an imaginative construct, ideas, language itself, or a combination of these. Critics of all sorts have found the metaphor serviceable, for it suggests the exercise of an active imagination. More specifically, it refers to the penetration of an area unknown or partly known, by one who tries to make sense of it, naming, examining, describing, comparing, relating it to what he already knows, and all the while moving deeper into it so as to possess it from within. I do not think we should be upset by the colonial, imperial, military and sexual

151

connotations which are certainly present, for, though I have no right to exploit others, I have every right to take full possession of my own mind's interior. I even have a duty to do it: I become the better for it, in that through it I can live more fully, and if I am good at it my readers can do so too, because the ultimate object is not of domination but of understanding.

> Pray thee, take care, that tak'st my book in hand,
> To read it well: that is, to understand,

says Ben Jonson, recognizing that "to understand" is the principal end of both writer and reader, and that reading is an imitation of the writer's activity.

Thirty years ago, George Dekker published a book about the *Cantos* entitled *Sailing after Knowledge*. I owe a great deal to it, because it helped me to work my way into the *Cantos* as nothing else had done. The title comes from Canto XLVII, and refers both to Odysseus and to the Poundian poet and explorer who, Dekker pointed out, followed a "periplum" rather than a map,

> periplum, not as land looks on a map
> but as sea bord seen by men sailing.

(Canto LIX)

What exploration *feels* like is to run into the sensory reality of something, often before even knowing what it is in conceptual terms, and almost always before being able to fit it in with the already known. The sailor rounds a point of land to face the next unforeseen feature of the coast he is traveling along; the speaker in Eliot's "Marina" moves into "scent of pine and the woodthrush singing through the fog"; Pound himself encounters the immediacy of jungle as "glaze green and red feathers" (Canto XX). And these are the ways in which we initially come into all of our knowledge, especially if we are poets writing in the first half of the twentieth century.

But it is precisely this kind of experience that Duncan would prefer to call adventure, emphasizing that, by not knowing what happens next, the traveler is constantly moving out of control. Of course, the concepts of exploration and adventure overlap, to an extent: for an explorer is bound to have adventures, since he has not been this way before; and conversely someone who adventures may be doing so as part of a wider enterprise, whether or not he plans it as such. Yet the meanings of the concepts are sufficiently distinct. Exploration is something you do to something else, as systematically as you can. Columbus or Livingstone or Lewis and Clark set out with certain general intentions of control and direction, even if those intentions miscarry on the way. But adventures happen *to* you, as they do to King Arthur's knights, or Fabrice del Dongo, or the Bastables. You don't know where the next one is coming from, unless it is to be set in motion by Morgan le Faye or the Muse, both of whom keep their own counsel. There is then a clear connection between adventure and spontaneity, a word Duncan rightly associated with the values of the Romantics.

The word exploration implies responsible and adult activity, as far as possible rational in its intentions—it is directed toward the future, in which a discovery is to be completed, and a new land added to the map of the understood. But the adventure is likely to be enjoyable in itself, it may evoke childlike wonder, and there are strong associations of randomness and fun: the adventure takes place in the present, for it could not have been foreseen, and has all the excitement of the unexpected. That is why children's books are full of adventures. Nevertheless, Gawayn and Fabrice were not children during their principal adventures, and in fact as adults we find ourselves continually having to deal with the unexpected.

It is true that Fabrice is still almost a child at Waterloo, in what might be called the first act of *The Charterhouse of Parma*. In it, he establishes a pattern which allies him even more closely with the knight-errant or fairy-tale hero (and of course he is like them a younger son), because in searching for the true battle, the genuine Waterloo (characteristically glimpsed through patches of fog), he is on a *quest*. That is, he is already the kind of person who will lead his life in a posture of readiness for adventure.

You might say that duplicity characterizes the very circumstances of adventure. "We made camp": that is one stage, perhaps, of an exploration. But "we landed on an island where we made camp, and then discovered that the island was really the back of Leviathan": that is adventure. Fabrice at Waterloo is present at both a real battle and an uncoordinated jumble of incidents. Gawayn cuts off a head which continues talking, and later he is required to accept and partially betray the hospitality of the head's owner, who is both affable companion and deadly enemy. The more duplicitous the circumstances, the better the adventure.

And since for Robert Duncan poetry was adventure, the more duplicitous *its* circumstances, the better the poem. Something else: Duncan had a physical predisposition to the duplicitous adventure, in that he literally saw double. As the result of a childhood accident, his eyes were crossed. His double vision was not the same as Blake's second sight, which appears to have been true hallucination; but it was real enough, and inevitably it was charged with metaphorical possibility:

> Crossd,
> the sinister eye sees the near
> as clear fact,
>   the far
> blurs; the right eye
>   fuses all that is
> immediate to sight.

Thus both visual duplicity *and* visual blur are Duncan's daily experience.

These lines come from "A Poem Slow Beginning," from which I have already quoted, appearing early in *The Opening of the Field*, his book of 1960 that is both a landmark in the poetry of our half-century and the best entrance into Duncan's mature work. The same book includes an *ars poetica*, "Poetry, a Natural Thing." Here he gives us two separate images for the poem itself, first as it appears to the composing poet, a process taking place, and then as it appears to the reader, an artifact like a picture. Let me take the second image first. The picture he shows us is a literal one, an oil-painting by Stubbs, of a moose: the moose is comic and rueful—old antlers on the ground, new antlers barely started—caught in mid-course antlerwise as it were, "his only beauty to be / all moose." A clear antecedent is to be found in the famous, almost too famous, definition of Marianne Moore's (which she unaccountably elected to place between quotation marks) that poets should present real toads in imaginary gardens. This, then, is the real moose in the artist's imaginary garden.

The difference is that, while the toads are complete toads, the moose is caught in a state of unfinishedness, and indeed the image follows the other apparently contrasting one in which we see poetry as an intense and driven *process,* in Romantic opposition to the orthodox-Modernist artifact. Instead of static oil-painting we have the vision of salmon "battling, inarticulate" at the falls, "a spiritual urgency at the dark ladders leaping." This last phrase is characteristic of Duncan's best writing, in which boldly vigorous concept and equally vigorous image combine by interpenetration. The beauty of the salmon is not that of the moose, for they are on a quest as surely as any Arthurian knight:

> This beauty is an inner persistence
>   toward the source
> striving against (within) down-rushet of the river.

"The source" is fraught with implication, and to reach it is a matter of life and death. But I need hardly say that it must be seen in two ways, for it is a truism with us, let alone salmon, that a source revisited is not the same as it was. To swim upstream is also a double activity, both going against the current and within it. (The very cumbersome air of improvisation to the last line might be taken as equivalent to the salmon's desperate awkwardness but—like it—is contained inside the "urgency" of the whole action.) Contradictions are of the essence, it being for Duncan "a natural thing" to live them through, in a poem or a life.

The last poem in the book, "Food for Fire, Food for Thought," is in itself a magnificent paradox, for how can there be a last poem when you believe in a form so open that there are no closures and so no last things possible in it? To the imagery of shifting clouds there are echoes of Prospero's farewell speech, to that of flames there are analogies of Pentecostal tongues, but at the center there is a group of images whose doubleness is more sharply limited—that is, they may be seen *either* precisely as A *or* precisely as B: "Leonardo saw figures that were stains upon a wall," Duncan tells us, and later he has someone (as if in an E. Nesbit story) invite us to see the "fairies of the fire" on the hearth. We find in fact large blurry Pentecostal ambiguities mingling here with sharper duplicities of vision; and the whole poem looks both backward and forward. Like the antlerless moose who may also be seen as a moose growing new antlers from its buds, so the flames which "at the edge of our belief bud forth" hold a promise of some greater fire in the future and also look back to the childhood "flowers [that] are flames" referred to in the first poem of the book.

Many a poem (and play and novel, for that matter) introduces opposed terms, which are eventually either reconciled or not reconciled. But opposed terms are not necessarily duplicit. When Shakespeare says, "Two loves I have, of comfort and despair," his terms are not duplicit. In Duncan's poetry, on the other hand, the situation is *deceptive:* for, rather than seeing two clearly stated alternatives like comfort and despair, he is likely to see one thing in two ways. Does he hear the words "by longing" or "belonging"? Is that a stain on the wall or the painting of a figure? Should he say the salmon are going against the stream or within it? In fact, he implies, he does not choose between such alternatives: he must keep them both in mind, hearing both, seeing both, saying both. The poet's presiding consciousness is all that holds the poem together, and it does so by balancing the opposed terms, by holding them both equal, and preserving them without destroying either in a false reconciliation.

Superficially, Pound's technique of "rhyming"—Helen of

Troy with Elinor of Aquitaine, Odysseus with the exploring poet—might look similar to what Duncan is doing. (It is also Eliot's technique in *The Waste Land,* of course, and Joyce's in *Ulysses,* and it is probably in *Ulysses,* as Ronald Bush suggests, that it originates.) But these are really *equivalent* figures, not duplicit ones; and it is important that they be considered distinct so that the rhyming has force. The mature Pound is able to conflate without blurring; but Duncan rejoices not only in the deceptiveness of the situation in which he finds himself but also in that blurring of the perception that often accompanies it. (What *do* I hear? What *do* I see?) It is Duncan's achievement that his poetic enterprise can on occasion successfully accommodate not only "rhyming," not only what he calls duplicity, but a luminous blur at its heart, an indistinctness that is still meaningful.

4

> [Fingal's Cave] was the first painting by Turner to go to the
> United States. After it remained unsold for thirteen years, C. R.
> Leslie chose it for James Lenox, whose first reaction was
> disappointment at its indistinctness. When Turner heard this he
> made the famous reply: "You should tell him that indistinctness is
> my forte."
>
> Graham Reynolds, *Turner*

Whatever the differences between them, Duncan took continued pride in his derivation from Pound, and consciously employed Poundian technique, most demonstrably perhaps in "A Poem Beginning with a Line by Pindar." Its structure is Modernist and collagist, resembling "not a statue but a mosaic" (to quote its own words). Items of "information" accumulate like the tiny fragments of stone that will make up the whole mosaic. It was perhaps the archaic method of Pindar; it is certainly the Poundian method, the quickest way to emphasize the rhyming between events, people, and ideas.

Nevertheless, we would hardly recognize Duncan's as a

Modernist poem from its first seven lines (the first of which, admittedly, is quoted from Pindar):

> *The light foot hears you and the brightness begins*
> god-step at the margins of thought,
>> quick adulterous tread at the heart.
> Who is it that goes there?
>> Where I see your quick face
> notes of an old music pace the air,
> torso-reverberations of a Grecian lyre.

The quotation is from C. M. Bowra's translation of the First Pythian Ode, of which it is the third line. It is easy to understand why it stuck in the poet's mind. "The líght fóot héars you and the bríghtness begíns." It seems to reproduce the pace of a measured listening at the same time as that of the measured footfall itself, followed by a slight hurry of reaction (of "poetic disturbance," to take a phrase from another book by Duncan). Moreover, in spite of a certain resemblance to the cadence of an Old English line, its rhythm, interwoven with alliteration and with unemphasized internal rhymes and half-rhymes, makes a music the more compelling because we do not recognize it as part of any pattern of scansion: its power seems extempore, and its melody constitutes something of an adventure for the ear, unforeseen and unplanned.

The sense of the line in original context is clear enough. The "you" is Apollo's lyre, heard by the leader of the Chorus, he of the light foot, who is both singer and dancer. A gloss on "brightness" is to be found in Bowra's introduction to his translation. The "divine force," he says, Pindar "commonly compares with light. . . . What Pindar conveys in song is precisely the enhancement of consciousness which his athletes enjoy in the moment of triumph."[9] The brightness, then, is sent by Apollo to the winner of the race, and to the Chorus, and to all those who are audience of the Ode.

But Duncan deliberately takes the line out of context, and gives us no antecedents to identify foot or god, much less adultery or face. There is a strong possibility of synesthesia, as if a foot might hear. (Or it could even be taken as a light foot metrically: meaning is up for grabs.) The quoted line in isolation suggests an unexpected disturbance, as in one wakening from sleep at the sudden onset of sexual desire. The light foot, its god-step, its tread and its pace, may be no more than the beating of the heart. "Who is it that goes there?" indeed, and whose is the "quick face"? (more synesthesia in that last phrase, probably, even though "quick" also means live). They are not identified, and all we can say is that they hint at the Platonic form of the Lover, though on a rereading of the poem we shall be able to recognize him as Cupid—the god who treads in the heartbeat, his face illuminated by the brightness of Psyche's lamp. But this is to read ahead, and meanwhile we are meant to be profusely bewildered: a barely identifiable excitement with many possible referents is conveyed to us with much rhetorical power. In fact, the speaker's voice is clear but his situation is unclear. The consequence is a poetry at the same time indistinct and energetic—words we might use of a Romantic painting by Turner, with a blur at its heart. The power is all in the suggestion, the fine cadences, the incomplete hints of emotion. What is more, the situation is not only blurred but duplicit as well, for we are plunged already in an adventure of which we do not know the name or nature. What on earth, the poet-reader-sailor wonders, is round the next point of land?

So the poem about yearning begins, with intimations as unlocalized as the first impulses of puberty. Then, with a Poundian juxtaposition that is in fact a pinpointing rather than a change of subject, Duncan introduces Goya's painting of Cupid and Psyche, and gives us a partial opportunity to localize some of the references, though with as yet little certainty. We next find various examples of *traditionally* duplicit devices—allegory and pun and paradox. Allegory: the two figures are not only characters adequate in themselves, but have always stood for the abstractions of Love and Soul, who here punningly "exist in an obscurity"—a literal darkness of background in the painting, and also an obscurity of purpose and of ultimate fate. Later there is another pun in "Psyche is preserved": she stays young, and she gets through her difficulties intact. And paradoxically, the two bodies "yield out of strength," as we all do while making love; and every incident in the story however disastrous "serves" the lovers. These devices may be traditional, but a bit later in the poem Duncan will play with and distort language in a "modern," Joycean way—"a phase" sounding like "aphasia" and "the present dented of the U / nighted stayd" being an aphasic resaying of "the president of the United States" that refers perhaps to a battered president, a benighted country, a situation that is stayed.

Duncan has referred to the lovers' eyes as "diffuse with rapture," and diffusion might be a word for describing what happens to the idea of yearning in the poem's course, for it is certainly (in dictionary terms) "poured or sent out so as to spread in all directions; spread abroad, circulated, permeated." That is what happens to brightness in Turner's paintings—it is diffused, in an intentional blur. Here meaning is diffused, but by using Poundian methods. Michael Davidson, in a faithful and penetrating account of the poem, says: "this first part . . . is an homage to the romance tradition in distinctly modernist terms. It inaugurates a mythic search for lost innocence within the folds of specific aesthetic artifacts."[10] The artifacts include Pindar's Ode, Goya's painting, Apuleius' tale, poems and prose by Whitman, the *Pisan Cantos*, and nineteenth-century American paintings of Western landscape. The searches include Psyche's for Cupid, Whitman's for the lost Lincoln, Jason's for the Fleece, and Pound's for—what? himself? balance? sanity? Each search in the poem, however, is charged with the feeling of Psyche's, which encloses all the others, and is driven by that erotic yearning that Duncan sees as proper to the soul. In the second section, taking off from Whitman's address of Lincoln as lost lover in "When Lilacs Last in the Dooryard Bloom'd," Duncan himself engages in a quest for the American president who will satisfy the heart's yearning. He starts intoning various litanies composed of the names of the presidents in sequence, going now forward in time and now backward, but each one breaking off, as if having nowhere to go, no name to dwell on lovingly:

> Hoover, Roosevelt, Truman, Eisenhower—
> where among these did the power reside
> that moves the heart? What flower of the nation
> bride-sweet broke to the whole rapture?

The Psyche-poet searches for the Eros-president in tetrameters half-trochaic and half-iambic: "flower" reminds us of Whitman's lilacs, and "rapture" of the lovers' eyes. I take lines like these as incident to Duncan's adventure of not knowing: for in them, a risk is taken, language is on the verge of gush, it courts uncontrol. The meter only emphasizes the closeness to cliché. Once again, as in the first seven lines of the poem, feelings are bewilderingly dominant.

But, Duncan continues, the presidents since Lincoln "dwell in the roots of the heart's rancor." Yearning for the brightness of flowers—with all the associations that have accumulated around the concept of brightness in this poem—he must descend instead into the darkness of roots, from rapture to rancor. It is a complex image, for roots are as essential as its blossoms to the whole plant. We must infer from it that rancor and darkness are as necessary to us as rapture and brightness; and, sure enough, the poem will insist later that the light of day which Jason seeks always "verges upon dark," the night with which it alternates. The Bad Presidents may then be as necessary to the nation's story as "jealousy, ignorance, the hurt" are to Psyche's.

He continues to move, backward now, through the litany of presidents:

> Hoover, Coolidge, Harding, Wilson
> hear the factories of human misery turning out commodities.
> For whom are the holy matins of the heart ringing?
> Noble men in the quiet of morning hear
> Indians singing the continent's violent requiem.
> Harding, Wilson, Taft, Roosevelt,
> idiots fumbling at the bride's door,
> hear the cries of men in meaningless debt and war.

I must say, I love this part. The incantatory power of the litany sustains the rather generalized but exalted language, which may well recall that of the prophetic Blake and the political Shelley. At the same time Duncan, for all his attraction to not-knowing, is also attracted to Dante, the great knower, and there-fore, is something of a categorizer. As he matches rapture and rancor, flower and root, so here he matches the matins by a requiem! And then we come to the striking line, "idiots fumbling at the bride's door," which in the compressed energy of its contempt and the active visual strength of its allegory brings the disparate elements of the entire passage together in a way worthy of Blake and Shelley at their best, in their role of vision-ary pamphleteers. The longer line that follows, relating the image of idiot-bridegroom back to the actual social troubles of the post–Civil War era, clinches that resemblance, admirably suggesting the crude urgency of political lampoon with its slightly doggerel effect. The passage demonstrates wonder-fully how bad writing (doggerel and trite language, for exam-ple) may "serve" the purposes of the whole poem in the same way that disasters serve Psyche's ultimate fortunes.

So Duncan as usual proceeds through deceptively symmetrical opposites, of style as of concept and image; and so, he insists, does his story, when he comes to the impossible labors set by Venus. "These are the old tasks," he says in an almost offhand tone (an eight-page poem has room for many changes of tone):

> They must be impossible. Psyche
> must despair, be brought to her
> > insect instructor

—for it is her friend the ant that will enable her to sort the seeds one from another, in the first of the tasks. "They must be impossible," *must* that is for the story, which is like that of the Fortunate Fall, for (in Michael Davidson's words) the soul may only come to "the discovery of desire through loss and restitution."[11] Or, as another put it, "without Contraries is no Progression."

Pound himself now enters the subject matter of the poem, as a yearner and light-bringer comparable to Psyche and Whitman:

> In the story the ants help. The old man at Pisa
>   mixd in whose mind
> (to draw the sorts) are all seeds
>   *as a lone ant from a broken ant-hill*
> had part restored by an insect, was
>   upheld by a lizard . . .

And here, appropriately enough, Duncan is most Poundian in his means of association, the Psyche-Pound rhyme hinging on the appearance of an ant in each story (though in fact the "insect" of the fifth line above refers to a wasp).

Now that the embracing idea of yearning from the depths of tribulation has been thoroughly established, it may be extended and deepened in the sensory detail of several quests, of Jason, who yearns for "the fleecy sun," or of American pioneers, Duncan's own forebears, who yearn to possess the West: but even here progression is made through contraries, for each moves toward the source of light indirectly, traveling Westward like those in Looking-Glass Land, who must walk away from a place in order to approach it.

It is a search still for the Platonic Beloved, who is himself a cluster of opposites. The oracle in the story referred to Cupid as a monster, and Duncan recognizes the monstrous side to love. Cupid is not the dimpled baby of Valentine cards, but "Serpent-Desire / that flies thru the air / a monster-husband," and also "Cupidinous Death." And Duncan touches down, comes to an apparent rest at the end of the poem's third quarter with a certain self-satisfied Romantic morbidity—it is for a moment as if he is *too* satisfied in a kind of hedonistic Ode-to-Melancholy way with the identification between Love and Death. "Cupidinous Death! / that will not take no for an answer," it ends. But we may rightly be suspicious of such complacency from one whose feeling through the poem thus far has been of vigorous restlessness, delighted with the unending imaginative process in which he takes part as he moves through "life after life."

If he needed, earlier, to qualify the brightness by reminding us of the darkness it verged, he needs now to qualify the darkness. This he does at once, by enthusiastically cutting through the snakelike coils of his melancholic knot with the "Oh yes!" that starts off the last section. After all, he had just paused on a double negative—and his affirmative is both a witty transposition of it and an answer to it. For the god-step is still sounding, more loudly than ever, in the ominous thuds of snow falling from a roof, which will eventually be transposed in their turn to the steps of the dreamed children in the field.

It is this, the image of playing children, that has started the entire book in which we read this poem, at the center of the book's commissioned title page and of the opening poem. The dance in the meadow is a visionary pun on Charles Olson's poetics of "composition by field," a field which is both an open and a boundaried place; and is thus not only an image in the poetry but an image for it as well.

The god-step coincides with that of the children at ring-around-the-roses as it did earlier with that of the Chorus dancing Pindar's Ode: their activity may be seen as both part of the quest and part of its fulfilment.

> *Finders Keepers* we sang
>   when we were children   or were taught to sing
>   before our histories began   and we began
>   who were beloved   our animal life
>   toward the Beloved, sworn to be Keepers.

Thus the soul seeks out the beloved in lifetime after lifetime, "station after station," from Pindar's archaic ceremonies to a children's game played today. The dream-vision binds the multiple stories of the poem together triumphantly. And it also delivers the poet from a literal night of reflection and writing, apparently, the light of his desk lamp now, like that of Psyche's oil lamp, lost in the greater brightness of a fulfilment:

> A line of Pindar
> moves from the area of my lamp
>   toward morning.
>
> In the dawn that is nowhere
>   I have seen the willful children
>
> clockwise and counter-clockwise turning.

They dance like the waves of the grass, we have been told, they move "to adore the mystery of Love" (he quotes from a hymn), like the adventuring troubadours, like the violent pioneers, like Jason. The texture of the poem is tight with the interrelationship of all the references. Jason "struggles east / widdershins to free the dawn": now the dawn is freed and the brightness begins; in the motion of their dance the children perpetuate opposites and balance them. And of course in such lines the poem reaches the ideal Duncan ending; for a closure in the midst of a process suggests that there is no real closure, only a withdrawal of the poet's attention.

5

Duncan's direction finally became clear with the publication of *The Opening of the Field* in his forty-first year. He had decided to be a poet of inclusiveness—writing poetry, that is, with room for everything he knew, as Dante had done, and Whitman, and Pound. Each of these poets spoke to him like a heroic teacher, but it was Pound's structural method—not Whitman's or Dante's—he chose to use in the most important poem of the book.

In feeling and tone he is a more consistently *personal* poet than Pound. He, Robert Duncan, addresses his reader as someone to be emotionally won over: thus he remarks that "the oracle at Miletus had spoken / truth surely" (I cannot imagine Pound saying "surely" in this way), and thus he exclaims "Oh yes!" (with an impetuous note foreign to the adult Pound). But even though his voice is distinct from the master's so often, he is able to speak with the authentic eloquence, that harmonious compression of essentials, which must make the *Cantos* the prime poetic model of the century:

> Scientia
> holding the lamp, driven by doubt;
> Eros naked in foreknowledge
> smiling in his sleep;   and the light
> spilld, burning his shoulder—the outrage
>   that conquers legend . . .

Any more condensation and it would be mere shorthand, but within the swiftly delineated outlines nothing is lost, and a life of dense detail is fully implied. (Chokeweed clogs up certain of Duncan's poems, but not this one.) Duncan adopts a Poundian style at its finest, then, besides quoting from him and introducing him as a character. And he uses his structural method the more appropriately because the Pindar poem is, like the *Cantos*, about a recurrence of pattern in history and art, a pattern here finely reanimated in the *un*Poundian image of playing children that ends the poem.

And the image is indeed unPoundian in its origins and purport: it results from a fusion of dream and memory, it shows us children wise in their wonder and innocence, and it celebrates not only pattern but impulsive life within that pattern. They are "willful children" (this is the regular American spelling, I should point out, which does not *necessarily* denote a difference from the English "wilful"), and share an unexamined spontaneity with the Western landscape of wilderness. Yet it is a spontaneity that has its own laws. To explain this statement I must touch on one of the most difficult paradoxes of Duncan's thought.

In the *Agenda* tribute to Pound of 1965, Duncan says:

> My concern with the nature of the Law was inspired and continues to be inspired by the poet of *The Cantos* who brought Kung into our studies, tho I derive from the concept that all order proceeds from and depends upon its roots in a man's inner order the politics of a lawful anarchism, Vanzetti's voluntarism, opposed to the politics of coercion, be it the "democracy" of majority rule or the "fascism" of Mussolini's dictatorship.[12]

Duncan normally took pains with his prose, revising it repeatedly. But, for whatever reason, the writing here is slipshod and confusing; so that when something is said to depend upon its root and syntax starts to dissolve and quotation marks are used to sweep away inconvenient problems, you are tempted to dismiss a phrase like "lawful anarchism" as double-talk—merely a way of saying "I have learned from Pound's ideas but I'm not a fascist." That would be a pity, though, for Duncan is here making a sharp distinction. Anarchism cannot be infinite, since our impulses are not all good. Self-destructiveness, for example, has to be checked somewhere, and that somewhere he calls the Law. Law, moreover, is connected with the concept of poetic "permission" alluded to in the opening words of the book, "Often I am permitted to return to a meadow." Both refer to a controlling power outside of him. Michael André Bernstein defines permission as "both signalling and confirming the entrance of every poet into his vocation," to explain later:

> The closest parallel I know to Duncan's understanding of "permission" . . . is the theological paradox of prayer in which the only appropriate blessing for which one should ask is grace and yet it is precisely grace that is required as a precondition of rightful prayer.[13]

I would further connect it, but more loosely, with the traditional idea of poetic inspiration, particularly as taken up by the Romantics and then by popular lore: inspiration comes from the Muse but it is still all your own.

The children are willful but their game implies *lawful* anarchism, in the same way that the poet writes spontaneously out of his own imagination but under Permission, and that improvised adventures are part of a quest—the law, the permission, and the quest each defining a parallel undertaking freely moved within which yet comes from outside. Like free will for a Calvinist, spontaneity within the law is the ultimate duplicit condition. It is difficult to conceptualize, but it becomes clear when we think of the law as equivalent to a children's game or dance, with its conventions, patterns, and rules so well learned that they are obeyed in behavior indistinguishable from true impulsiveness.

What is more, Duncan himself is *stylistically* willful within the defined subject, or quest, of the poem. As the indistinct writing of the opening lines is followed by the distinctness of the description of Goya's painting, or as the blurred Romantic lushness of the rhetorical questions in the middle of the second section are cut into by the devastating precision of the remark about the idiot-bridegroom, so he validates out-of-

167

control and self-indulgent writing by giving it a place in the embracing scheme.[14] The grass grows freely within the shadowy boundaries of the field.

At first Duncan thought of himself as a Modernist, and later as a Romantic. Actually, as he came to realize, he was both all along, but it must have been a difficult recognition to make because of the antagonism to the Romantics so often expressed by the Modernists, especially by Pound and Eliot. Finally in possession of his greatest powers, he brought about a marriage between Modernism and Romanticism—a marriage considered impossible before it took place. He built on Pound, and did so in unexpected ways, not only by imitating "the sublime and ecstatic" side of him, but also by combining his influence with that of Romantic poets like Blake and Whitman, marrying him to the very poetry he had rejected.[15] To put it in another way, Duncan pursued the intellectual adventure of not knowing, but according to Modernist methods.

The only other poem of our half-century that I would place in the same class as the Pindar poem is Basil Bunting's *Briggflatts*. It too is a personal enterprise, in no narrow sense, being both "an autobiography" and a quest. In design and detail it surpasses even Duncan's achievement, I believe, but it is similar to it in its mix of derivations. Again it is a marriage of Modernist and Romantic possibilities, the difference being that what Bunting unites with Pound is Wordsworth, another rejected poet ("a silly old sheep with a genius"). Both Duncan and Bunting avoid the twin vices of trivialization that in their different ways haunt the English and American poetry of our time: the use of anecdotal subject matter as an end in itself and of technical play as an end in itself. (I take it that Hardy and Williams are behind the one, Stein and Auden behind the other.) They are ambitious enough to pursue exalted themes with passionate feeling. Independently, in the strength of their talent and intelligence and dedication, they have invented a new poetry, moving and meaningful, out of the old elements. They deserve our prolonged attention, and the intensive study which will come from our delight.

NOTES

1. Robert Duncan, "The Lasting Contribution of Ezra Pound," *Agenda* 4, no. 2 (October–November 1965): 23.

2. From an interview in *Boundary 2*, quoted in Ekbert Faas, *Young Robert Duncan* (Santa Barbara, Calif.: Black Sparrow, 1983), p. 241.

3. Basil Bunting, "Mr. Ezra Pound," *The New English Weekly*, (1932); reprinted in *Basil Bunting: Man and Poet*, ed. Carroll F. Terrell (Orono, Maine: National Poetry Foundation, 1981), p. 254.

4. Kenneth Cox's characteristically succinct and practical account of the *Cantos* (*PN Review* 72 [1989]: 12–13) warns of the risk in using the term juxtaposition of Pound's structural method. "Without being made explicit," he says, "the view presented by the frequent and inconsiderate use of the word is that the composition of the Cantos is haphazard." Yes, I agree, so I shall try to use it infrequently and considerately; but I shall continue to do so because the effect of juxtaposition in Pound is surely meant to be, on each first encounter, *as if* haphazard. The technique of doing away with connections is used because the poet sees all his subjects as being in the end related—part of one big subject: and after our initial shock we are supposed to work out the connections for ourselves, whether they are of "consecutivity" (Cox) or simultaneity, contrast or similarity, linkage or collision. Apparent haphazardness is an essential part of the effect. (I here make use of the terms in a sentence from Joseph McElroy's *Lookout Cartridge* [New York: Carroll and Graf, 1985, p. 227]: "Pudovkin said montage was linkage, Eisenstein collision.")

5. John Pettigrew, notes to *The Poems*, by Robert Browning (New Haven: Yale University Press, 1981), vol. 1, p. 1043.

6. Ronald Bush, *The Genesis of Ezra Pound's Cantos* (Princeton: Princeton University Press, 1989), p. 80.

7. Robert Duncan, *Fictive Certainties* (New York: New Directions, 1985), p. 46.

8. Ibid., p. 2.

9. C. M. Bowra, *The Odes of Pindar* (Harmondsworth, U.K.: Penguin, 1985), p. xvi.

10. Michael Davidson, *The San Francisco Renaissance* (Cambridge: Cambridge University Press, 1990), p. 144.

11. Ibid., p. 142.

12. *Agenda*, p. 23.

13. Michael André Bernstein, "Bringing It All Back Home: Deri-

vations and Quotations in Robert Duncan and the Poundian Tradition," *Sagetrieb* 1, no. 2 (Fall, 1982): 181–82.

14. The same kind of validation takes place in his career as a whole. I heard him once in a poetry reading remarking how close some of his own writing may come to that of someone like Edna St. Vincent Millay. He does not therefore renounce that side of himself: if he is to be an inclusive poet, he must include this sort of thing too.

15. Pound's poem "A Pact" (1913) is a misleading poem, I believe. He is here addressing Whitman as a precursor in the writing of free verse. He also came to like the populist American side of Whitman; but I cannot imagine him having any time for "Song of Myself" sections 24 and 28, which most closely distinguish the kind of inclusive poet Whitman is.

III

Christopher Isherwood
Getting Things Right

1

When I first met Christopher Isherwood he was fifty and I was twenty-five, but I never for a moment felt that he was twice my age. We immediately started speaking together like long-time friends who hadn't met in years. He was tanned and youthful-looking, the famous bright eyes alert and observant; he perfectly adapted himself to his listener; his conversation was enthusiastic, lively, funny; and I said to myself, *this* is the way I want to age.

Gore Vidal has recorded lunching with him at MGM during the filming of *Diane*, a movie nobody ever saw, and this was the same summer, 1955. After we had talked for a while, Isherwood took me on the set, where I was eventually introduced to two of the leads, Roger Moore and Marisa Pavan, the King and Queen of France. I was not introduced to Lana Turner, who played Diane de Poitiers and, when visible at all, was kept at a star's distance, hedged in by attendants. Isherwood had warned me that he would have to leave me from time to time, but I was engrossed in watching the repeated takes of a short scene. It look place during an elaborate court banquet on tables forming three sides of a square, at the head of which the King, standing gallantly behind Diane, had to lean over and spear a strawberry with a fork to pop into her

First appeared as "Getting Things Right," *Threepenny Review* 42 (Summer 1990).

mouth. It went wrong again and again—now he missed the strawberry, now he dropped it, and each time before the scene was shot, even though Lana Turner had not been touched, her makeup man reappeared, fussing over her as if she had been in a pillow fight. It was all fascinating, and just what I had hoped for. She submitted her face to him, like the actress in *Prater Violet*, "as impersonally as one extends a shoe to the bootblack." Isherwood joined me for a moment, and left me again. I noticed then, among the others watching, a boy of about my own age who looked as if he had gone to school on a beach. I assumed he must work here. He apparently assumed the same about me, because he came over and quietly asked me what I was doing. I let it be known, with perhaps a degree too much casualness, that I was a friend of the scriptwriter. He had climbed over the studio walls, he said, and slipped onto the set in search of a job in movies, and could I help him?— anything would do. I promised I would introduce him to my friend, and did, but Isherwood, though warm as ever, told him at once that he had no influence of that sort. He was amazed at the boy's exploit. On the way to lunch he told me how difficult it was for an outsider to penetrate a set like this: the walls were high and the lot was crawling with guards. But though he was sorry not to be of help, it all crowned the morning, for this was the way life was supposed to be in a movie studio. It was like an incident from a Hollywood movie about Hollywood—or like Lana Turner herself being spotted by a talent scout, so many years ago, an unknown girl sitting at the soda fountain in Schwab's; and Isherwood was full of glee that he had provided the opportunity for it all. In the commissary I recognized a satisfactory number of famous faces, and we went on talking.

I felt free to bring up anything. This was the end of the McCarthy era, and I asked him if he had ever had any difficulties because of his own past politics. Not really, he said; at one time he had been visited by two FBI agents, who had behaved with circumspection. "And I told them everything about myself. But I did point out to them that the Left had flirted with Communism just as the Right had flirted with Fascism." Such a remark was unanswerable, of course, because true, and was a just commentary on the politics of the 1930s. He was not questioned any further on the matter. It must have been convenient for him as well that the narrators of his books had been almost as guarded about politics as they were about sex. They *flirted* indeed.

It was perhaps at this time that I asked him which he considered his best book. He didn't seem to think my question stupid but said at once, "The journals I kept throughout the forties, but they are safe in the Library of Congress and no one can get at them till after my death." (Later he withdrew them for use in the writing of *Down There on a Visit* and his autobiography.) I was surprised, but then, I hadn't read the journals, and figured that perhaps he was like Sickert, who valued the spontaneity of his sketches more than his canvases.

A friend asked him, on a later occasion, "What happened to Sally Bowles?" I thought my friend's question rather crude—hadn't he heard of *artistic creation?*—but Isherwood was delighted to tell him about what Jean Ross, the original of Sally, had gone on to do ("and now she's worried because her daughter is running wild!"). He was entirely without pretension or literary snobbery. For him there was no opposition between the art of the novel and that of the memoir. It was a question, I think, of the spirit in which the writer undertook his work: both arts shared the same end, which was of getting things right, and if the novelist invented and rearranged, it was with the object of making the shape of the record clearer and finally truer to the essentials of the original experience.

Though he lived in Los Angeles and I was to settle in San Francisco, I was to meet Isherwood many times during the next thirty years, usually with his lover, Don, and mine, Mike, and sometimes with the famous people he had asked to dinner. His novels had meant a lot to me before we met, but knowing him I was especially impressed by the at the time uncommon ease, casualness, and openness with which he carried his homosexuality. And of course he, like I, was an Englishman who lived in California, in love with his new home, and in a state of ambivalence toward his old. I had an irrational terror that on some visit back to England I might fall fatally ill, get *stuck* there, and die there without being able to return to America first. It was absurdly romantic, since my health was sturdy—yet it was a real fear, nevertheless, as though I would by dying there get wedged forever inside a purgatory of dissatisfied adolescence. I asked Isherwood once if he ever himself felt a similar fear. "Oh yes!" he said, "then my mother would have won!" But he said it with such a cheerfully melodramatic tone, as if guying a past self, that I couldn't tell how to take it.

In his company I remember myself as several times giving way to a pertness, amounting to rudeness, especially when speaking about people I had met at his house. I remember it with mortification. I was no teenager, after all. Was I trying, by this means, to show that I was a free spirit unbound by the conventions, to establish my comparative youthfulness (and so attractiveness, perhaps), and restore the difference between generations he had so completely and generously disregarded on our first meeting? That's the only way I can explain it. He, however, was forbearing with me, though remarks I let drop—about Cecil Beaton, whom I later came to like a lot, and about William Inge—clearly annoyed him, and rightly so, for their sheer discourtesy.

But for a while, until it was clear that I had rather outworn my original charm, I did naïvely feel that I must be one of Isherwood's best friends, he seemed so pleased to see me and he gave me so much pleasure by *his* company. I wasn't, of course; in fact there were hundreds of people who knew him as well as I, and many who were far closer—I was really on the peripheral rim of his acquaintance; but one night, in the booth of a restaurant-bar in Santa Monica, about 1972, I was able to understand why I had felt so. There were several of us present, and I found myself at one point watching him talk with the wife of a sound-man for a BBC documentary he had just completed. I noticed the way he devoted himself *wholly* to his interlocutor. The rest of us do not, we divide our attention, however politely, our eyes straying to the distractions of the background, but that undivided concentration of attentiveness that Isherwood turned on you ("Yes! Yes!" he would say eagerly) was without equal in my experience. He met you as you were seldom met by others.

Late in the 1970s he made a good many public appearances, on TV or in front of live audiences. I was present at one in 1979, when he spoke before an enormous, largely gay crowd, and I was interested that the passages he read by way of a preface were two that I most admired, one from the "Berlin Diary" sections of *Goodbye to Berlin,* and the other from the concluding pages of *A Single Man.* They did not take up much time, however, and for the most part of the program he answered a variety of questions from the audience, doing so at length, with spontaneity and untiring courtesy. I couldn't help noticing how he had at last aged—he was seventy-six then, after all—a stockiness of bearing having replaced the earlier wiry vigor. He now had the thickened neck and the stiff deportment I associated with the retired English military officer. (Poor man, he probably had a touch of arthritis.)

When I next met him I asked him if he were ever self-conscious doing this kind of thing. "No," he said brightly, "I seem to get the opposite to stage fright." He was *on* in public, in the same way that he could be in private, the public and private manner being on occasion identical—enthusiastic yet confiding, frank yet with a touch of the formal suggested perhaps by the very degree of articulateness. Indeed, he reminds us several times in his writings that he is a "play actor" by nature; and when later, in my last meetings with him, I thought he seemed somewhat out of it, drifting a little, lacking the old intensity to the point of vagueness, it did cross my mind that perhaps he was playing the part of "old man" for the sheer comedy of it. He was not in fact, he had cancer, and was subject to memory lapses by now, I learned from Don after his death; but even in this condition he could be disconcertingly aware that he was unaware, and in an interview with Armistead Maupin remarked of himself, "Yes, the whole of the East Wing has gone dark, I'm afraid," a wonderfully Mortmere joke to make about his own failing powers.

If he was both a performer and someone capable of giving you that supreme spontaneous attentiveness, all it means is that he was not a simple man, as you might already have guessed from his books. The attentiveness, after all, was not something he was born with; rather, it was a habit that he had perfected, much as an actor perfects the habits of his art. But it was not only a discipline that overflowed from the training of the novelist. It was also a form of spiritual courtesy, and courtesy is something that always has to be learned, since we start off as mere selfish babies.

Standing on that platform in San Francisco he had spoken as naturally and unforcedly as if he were speaking to me still in the MGM commissary. He did not leap to distinguish between public and private topics. Once, in my pert aspect, I had made some derogatory remark about the looks of Auden, whom I had met only as an elderly man, his face a map of lighter and deeper cross-hatchings. Oh, but he was so attractive as a young man, Isherwood hastened to tell me. "!?" I responded. "Oh yes, for years we fucked like rabbits every chance we got," he said, and that was a surprise to me, because I had always thought of their friendship as being strictly *literary*. (It came also as a surprise to their friend John Lehmann, as he has recorded.)

Isherwood was not indiscriminate, however: there was still a line between public and private when it was necessary. He did not like it when Allen Ginsberg's entourage started taping his private conversation once without his knowledge or permission, but that of course involved a betrayal of trust also. ("Somebody was saying 'Did you ever *sleep* with Gore Vidal?' and I suddenly became conscious of this little *thing*, this *machine*, whirring amongst them on the floor by the radiator . . .") He gave of himself widely, it was part of his great charm that he should do so, but he was not going to let himself be exploited. It was sometimes necessary to defend one's privacy, as it was also necessary to keep one's work hours free. "I make it easy for people to visit me," he said, "—the first time." Putting in the work was important, and he wasn't going to become a Truman Capote wasting his days in gossip and literary chitchat instead of writing. As he got older he seemed to become more and more aware that he had little time left to complete what he had projected. The third volume of his autobiography would have dealt, I believe, with the secular side of his early years in Los Angeles, and they would have made absorbing reading. "You actually knew Garbo?" I once

xclaimed. "Oh yes," he said, "I knew her probably as well as
nyone in the world did—which wasn't much."—And he used
o go to a gym at which the young, unknown Ryan O'Neill
vorked out with his even handsomer brother. (It was the
rother they all expected to become a star.)—I should have
sked him about such things in more detail, I should have
aken notes—he would have told me, as he would have told
nyone; I should have asked him about meeting Chaplin, for
xample, and Brecht, in those early years—what were those
luplicitous and difficult geniuses really like?

Well, presumably the last volume was never written, but
here are the collected journals to look forward to. I hear that
hey have found their ideal editor, so we may expect them to
tart appearing in print a few years from now. Meanwhile we
nay reread.

2

In the middle of writing this essay, I am sent a new book,
Where Joy Resides, described as "a Christopher Isherwood
Reader" and edited by Don Bachardy and James P. White. I
am normally suspicious of "readers"—think of *The Marianne
Moore Reader,* available in secondhand bookstores everywhere!
They are usually nothing more than handsome gift books, full
of snippets and incompletions, easy-reading "samplers" (another word to be wary of) for the real thing. But this, though
admittedly handsomely produced, is in effect a Selected
Works, and a good one at that. Isherwood gives himself especially well to selection, since most of his fiction takes the form
of novellas, of which it is possible to fit quite a few into a large
book like this. It contains—from *Goodbye to Berlin*—the first
"Berlin Diary" and "Sally Bowles" (originally published on its
own), and all of *Prater Violet,* "Mr. Lancaster" (the best part of
Down There on a Visit), and *A Single Man.* It also includes six
reviews and essays and some tastes from *Kathleen and Frank,
Lions and Shadows,* and *My Guru and His Disciple.* Isherwood is
hardly an inaccessible writer, but this collection would make as
balanced an introduction to his work as you could imagine,

and I only demur at the presence of the reviews (he was
competent reviewer, but in no way special). There is also a fin
introduction by Gore Vidal, which reproduces and summa
rizes material from his longer essay of 1976 but makes som
additions, among which is a sparkling deathbed anecdote.

In looking through the collection I am forcibly reminde
about the primacy of memoir for Isherwood. He could sa
like Tolstoy that hardly a character or event in his fiction wa
completely fabricated. Not only did Sally Bowles have he
original, but minor characters like poor Ruthie in *Down Ther
on a Visit* (Cyril Connolly's first wife) or Grant Lefanu, th
physics professor in *A Single Man* (the late poet Henri Co
lette). He consciously and continually interpenetrated his fi
tion with his own literal experiences. I started this essay (a
Vidal started his) with a personal memoir, because I conside
that the qualities he worked for in his behavior were exactl
those he worked for in his writings. In those, from early o
intensity of attention is married to a comparatively relaxe
tone of voice. Thus in *Lions and Shadows* (1938), he describe
the operating theater in a hospital:

> [It] was like an unnaturally clean kitchen. And the nurses and
> dressers were like cooks, in their white caps, goloshes and sex-
> less overalls, chatting in groups, or scrubbing their hands at
> the sink, or busy at the gleaming silver oven doors of the steril-
> izers. The air was steamy. The atmosphere was expectant, yet
> somehow horribly domestic.

The first three sentences, one long one carefully placed be
tween two short, would not be out of place in *The Sentiment
Education,* with their spare selection of crisp physical detai
their telling use of a sustained analogy, and their economy o
summation. But the fourth sentence breaks up the implie
formality, for "horribly," unlike every other word here, is reck
lessly imprecise. Isherwood is fond of similar adverbs lik
"absurdly" and "terribly," and always they are there for th
sake of the tone, which as a result becomes gossippy and off
hand, making the whole scene more accessible, putting th
reader at ease. Vidal has noted the similar effect Isherwoo

gets from the strategic introduction of the second person: it brings the reader in.

But for all the informality, for all the ease and lightness, for all the air of having words to waste, Isherwood's prose is written with an unremitting control. His analogies are never decorative, but on the contrary severely functional—how often they belittle grandeur, domesticate the exotic, or make violence appear ordinary (the lesson he learned from Forster). "At the end of [the street], like a tall, dangerously sharp, red instrument, stood a church," he tells us in *Goodbye to Berlin*. Berlin is full of everyday knives that can be put to murderous use. Such a short sentence dramatizes the full complexity of a time and place, the ominous sense of a bad future latent in a troubled present, and the wariness and suspiciousness of the narrator. His prose is a lucid medium for the transmission of situation, character, state of mind, and idea, and for all its succinctness shows how they intersect, crisscross, connect, or get in each other's way. Simple though it appears on first reading, we come to realize that it does not simplify.

A colloquial directness of style has been around since the early eighteenth century, but Isherwood's particular development of it is admirable because it is so varied in the uses to which it may be put: it can handle the most banal of experiences and it is also capable of eloquence, as I shall show. It is in the nature of a bequest to us—like the plain-style of the Elizabethan poets, it is useful for any subject matter, flexible and all-purpose as it is. And it is a real bequest, for though like most styles it is easy to imitate, like few others it is not a web of mannerisms. You write like Joyce or Proust or James at your peril, but nobody is likely to notice if you write like Isherwood, because you are directing the reader straight to the subject matter, as if style were no intermediary.

Transparency of style is not universally admired, I find. There is no need to pay attention to the view that writing so easy cannot be good, since that is merely the snobbery of the half-educated. But Isherwood's prose has not been much valued by the reigning critics of either his generation or mine. The New Critics, at whom we sneer nowadays (as if everything had changed!), were interested, rather, in "ambiguity," "irony," and "paradox," that is in the strategies of indirection and elaboration by which, it was implied, only a complicated style could transmit a complicated subject. The prestigious critics of today are interested in "indeterminacy" and writing that subverts itself: nor is solipsistic confusion frowned upon. Portentousness, jargon, imprecision, and mannerism are widely accepted and imitated in literary criticism now—and Isherwood's kind of transparency, since it clearly springs from a rigorous authorial control, is therefore to be considered authoritarian, thus reactionary, thus fascist. Yet it must have its admirers. It is so obviously practical in getting the job done, in creating meanings at the same moment that it conveys them, that the inheritance is not after all going to waste even though it comes in for so little official recognition. I detect its use in the writing of, for example, the fine first pages of Alan Hollinghurst's *The Swimming Pool Library,* which—without looking derivative for a moment—combines the power of objective perception with that of a subjective ease very much as in Isherwood.

For such a style is built on the assumption that objectivity is a desirable pursuit. Too much has been made of his phrase "I am a camera," as Isherwood himself knew, but nevertheless— given the fact that humans are creatures of almost uncontrollable bias—a camera is not a bad thing to emulate. Even the practice of analogy is not completely uncameralike: cameras often record that one thing resembles another, a church is like a knife, for instance, or foam on a brown stream like stout. The attempt to represent with clarity is always worth making, however impossible it is to achieve in absolute terms. (We may call the attempt "fairness.") There is no danger of the writer's ever turning into a real camera, but the imitation of a camera may be good training. And its faithfulness of attention to physical imagery is valuable because through it we may learn about the appearance of the world outside of us, or in other words about things we didn't know before. Doing so helps us to escape from the singleness of our own minds which, if lived in exclusively, become prisons.

I remember the publication of John Rechy's *City of Night* in the early 1960s, which had a considerable *succès de scandale* and is indeed still available. It was an account of what it is like to be a male prostitute who frequents a number of gay bars. It was an extraordinary chance to explore completely new ground, the subject matter of a stylized but subtly variegated society that, because of censorship problems, had been barely touched in print. It might have been as revealing as *Moll Flanders* or Mayhew's *London*, detailing the social customs, the manners and rituals, the traditions and absurdities and bravados and braveries, of an unfamiliar subculture in the heterosexual midst, one crowded with adaptive humans doing as well as they could, mostly, among rather odd circumstances. Alas, Rechy threw the chance away, concentrating on the reactions of his representative, the self-regarding hustler, instead of the things he was reacting to. Never were Isherwood's virtues more needed and never were they less in evidence.

Such an objective picture as he might have drawn, but of the very different bars of Berlin in about 1930, is one of the ingredients Isherwood would have liked to include in what became the Berlin books but, because homosexuality was a taboo subject then, the nature of the subculture had to be disguised and encoded. In any case, there was a great deal else from his life in Berlin that Isherwood wished to include.

He had already published one mature novel, *The Memorial*, which is somehow a difficult book to like. It certainly convinces, as a chronicle of the English gentry during the 1920s, and is in addition lively, dramatic, and readable. But, while it is full of rather unfriendly irony, it lacks that essential touch of the ridiculous which characterizes Isherwood's best work and seems to be connected with the presence of a first-person narrator (he is able to make fun of himself: for Isherwood the ridiculous begins at home). This novel, lacking such a personal viewpoint, takes its own sense of the representative a shade too seriously; it is almost schematic.

Isherwood has often told how he had planned to use all the Berlin material in an immense, elaborately structured novel to be called *The Lost*. (In *Christopher and His Kind*, he even offers a scenario he considered using.) Reading *The Memorial*, you can well imagine how it would have turned out: the portrait not of a family this time, but of a doomed society, heavy with drama, clotted with significance, and obedient to the multiple dictates of its ambitious title. But luckily the plot became too congested for him to handle, the characters "couldn't move without getting in each other's way"; so he first of all detached the Mr. Norris material for one short novel, and then at the urging of John Lehmann (the editor of *New Writing,* who was also the instigator of Orwell's career as an essayist) turned the best of the remainder into a series of loosely linked and even shorter narratives. By his inability to do the conventional thing he created his real abilities. It was not that the form of *Goodbye to Berlin,* as the second book ended by becoming, was in itself that new (in a way it is rather similar to Mrs. Gaskell's *Cranford,* or even late-picaresque novels like *Pickwick,* likewise conceived around a society or a group of acquaintances), but that its widespread subject matter is concentrated by the pressure of history. More of that in a minute; but equally important, at the center of it all, is a distinctive narrator: for here in the Berlin stories, in Gore Vidal's phrase, "Isherwood invented Isherwood."

The narrator of these early books is interesting almost to the extent that he is difficult to describe. (I can't help thinking of somebody in a dark bar who, in John Lennon's words, has "got to be good-looking 'cause he's so hard to see.") The literary device of his reticence or, as Isherwood later called it, his "evasiveness," becomes an aspect of character. As earlier noted, he flirts with communism as he does with what his author liked to call his queerness, not committing himself. He is the precise opposite of Rechy's narrator who, the object of desire, positively desires himself. Isherwood's narrator is self-effacing, as if he feels incomplete, but he is fascinated by others. He is one of those people who needs the presence of others to complete him—and they do, giving him so much substance that on occasion he is able to criticize his weaknessess without mercy and make fun of himself. The result is that, quite as much as the Berlin of the title, it is he who tactfully and modestly holds the book together, all the more because a good deal of his specificity is implied rather than given.

The other characters in the books are just the reverse. They are at once sharply individual and casually representative of a time and place. The book is inventive and unpredictable *in continual relation* to the historical record already known to the reader. (When it was first published, Hitler had been in power for six years.) Free agents, they think, but their actions take place in a kind of dance with history, sometimes evading it, sometimes forcibly led by it. A peculiar poignancy and strength is given to the writing by this aspect, then. Isherwood takes on not only the journalistic and fictional tasks of conveying what it is like to be in a particular place at a particular time, but the wider one as well, seeing it from a certain distance, and in its supreme manifestations the writing would be difficult to equal. Its scope may be seen from the start of the last section, entitled like the first "A Berlin Diary":

> To-night, for the first time this winter, it is very cold. The dead cold grips the town in utter silence, like the silence of intense midday summer heat. In the cold the town seems actually to contract, to dwindle to a small black dot, scarcely larger than hundreds of other dots, isolated and hard to find, on the enormous European map. Outside, in the night, beyond the last new-built blocks of concrete flats, where the streets end in frozen allotment gardens, are the Prussian plains. You can feel them all round you, to-night, creeping in upon the city, like an immense waste of unhomely ocean—sprinkled with leafless copses and ice-lakes and tiny villages which are remembered only as the outlandish names of battlefields in half-forgotten wars. Berlin is a skeleton which aches in the cold: it is my own skeleton aching. I feel in my bones the sharp ache of the frost in the girders of the overhead railway, in the ironwork of balconies, in bridges, tramlines, lamp-standards, latrines. The iron throbs and shrinks, the stone and the bricks ache dully, the plaster is numb.

Cold is felt here as a physical and immediate presence, overpowering the innumerable things named—the passage is crowded with *things*. The sensory force of the writing is such as to chill the reader in sympathy. It diminishes our small reserves of warmth, and thus takes from our humanness. The contraction of the cold is to an abstraction, to a *small* dot on the map which seems by reaction to have grown suddenly more *enormous*. The fact that the image of the map of Europe, the vast aerial survey, is a favorite one of the 1930s, and particularly of Isherwood's friend Auden, does not take from its effectiveness for a moment. The surveying agent, let us call it a movie camera now, comes in closer, to the plains, an ocean in which you could never make a home, dotted with forgotten battlefields—we are as helpless before the forces of history as we are before those of geography and of the seasons. The agent zooms in to even closer detail. Berlin is a skeleton—and the whole paragraph pivots on a colon, in which we swing round from the metallic skeleton of the city cold with winter to "my" skeleton cold with discouragement, dispiritedness, despair.

There is magnificence in the identification, its claim justified both by the cunning of the apparently plain writing and also by its context in the book as a whole. For the narrator has throughout been at the same time separated from his surroundings and identified with them. His degree of separation and his degree of identification have been the great secret subject of the Berlin stories. Here the Englishman realizes just how far he has become part of Berlin shortly before he leaves it, virtually for good.

In the next paragraph he goes on to speak about the two official centers of Berlin: and then in a third paragraph he changes the word "center" to its apparent synonym "heart"— the heart within a freezing skeleton:

> But the real heart of Berlin is a small damp black wood—the Tiergarten. At this time of the year, the cold begins to drive the peasant boys out of their tiny unprotected villages into the city, to look for food, and work. But the city, which glowed so brightly and invitingly in the night sky above the plains, is cold and cruel and dead. Its warmth is an illusion, a mirage of the winter desert. It will not receive these boys. It has nothing to give. The cold drives them out of its streets, into the wood which is its cruel heart. And there they cower on benches, to starve and freeze, and dream of their faraway cottage stoves.

This metaphor does not diminish or domesticate; rather, it does the opposite. The skeleton is a kind of zombie—it is dead, cold in both senses, and where its heart would be is a cruel absence. The boys freezing on their benches dream of cozy Grimms' fairy-tale cottages, but they are at the mercy of the "unhomely." This paragraph enacts no sentimental gesture, but takes its place firmly in the action of the book; for these are the boys who will now go on to the bars of the Alexanderplatz and from there to the S.A.—compelled to be other than themselves because outside forces have driven them.

This is surely as good prose as has been written in our time. For all its plainness, it has its own defined and various rhythms, rhythms difficult to separate from the sense. The interlocking complexities of situation, from that of a continent to that of an individual, are not subsumed by its clarity but conveyed by it. A steady attentiveness has brought Isherwood here: he in effect summarizes, but in his summary nothing is lost. Through the transparent medium, each thing, each person presented, is granted its own dignity.

3

Isherwood's fame is still based largely on the Berlin stories, and probably will continue to be so. That is as it should be: the best known is "Sally Bowles," which it seems can run through as many variations as the story of Antigone, and still be the same in essentials. No matter that in one version the narrator becomes heterosexual and in another bisexual, no matter that Sally, originally described as singing "badly, without expression," is played by Liza Minelli of the robust vocal delivery. Sally has grown greater than her book, joining other mythological characters like Cyrano and Mrs. Gamp and Falstaff, who also have floated free of their original contexts. A myth leads its own life.

Goodbye to Berlin was published in 1939, the year Isherwood emigrated to the United States. Once there, he changed. On the dust jacket of his next novel, *Prater Violet* (1945), his publishers, Random House, summarized—and dramatized—the change.

> Christopher Isherwood went into virtual literary retirement after [the Berlin] books were issued and . . . devoted himself to mystical studies while living monastically in Hollywood. He became a disciple of the Vedanta Society, a cult whose philosophy derives from the ancient Indian scriptures, the *Vedas*. As co-translator of *Bhagavad-Gita, The Song of God,* Christopher Isherwood has made a genuine contribution to the understanding of religious teachings considered by many as almost too occult for the Western mind.

Glibly as it may read, the account errs only in making the conversion sound perfected. Almost too occult though they may have been for our pitiful Western understandings, Isherwood's religious concerns were nevertheless to dominate his writing for the next forty years, either directly in the commissioned life of Ramakrishna and the essays (one of which he himself admitted read "like the parish magazine"), or indirectly, as in a fiction like *A Single Man,* which seems at first to be as unreligious as *Alice in Wonderland.*

His last book, *My Guru and His Disciple* (1980), is a sufficient corrective to the smugness of the *Prater Violet* blurb, being the record of his dealings with Vedanta, of his religious needs, of his attempts to lead a good life, and of all the hesitations, reversions, and inconsistencies that accompanied them. It reads rather like casual conversation, and is so laconic in tone that I didn't recognize it for the achievement it is until I came to read it a second time. It seems artless, but Isherwood was never artless. Rather, he had become a master of self-concealing artfulness.

The book is the more unified by its being the story of a love affair, a spiritual one, between Isherwood and the Swami Prabhavananda. The character of the Swami, in all its credible complexity and attractiveness, is an accomplishment that ranks with that of Sally Bowles, though it is doubtful that a musical will ever by made about *him.* He is a saint, as Auden grudgingly admitted, an unexpected and understated one, his religion defined not in abstract terms but as if inadvertently through his actions and words. To speak of him so, however, is also to speak of the book's method, which is, precisely, that of presenting beliefs exemplified and embodied as if inadvertently. Of course, what the Swami appears so casually may be part of a deep plan. Is it part of the plan that he seems to improvise, or is it part of the improvisation that he seems to plan? The same question, which is unanswerable, may be asked about the design and carrying-out of the book. It may be, further, that words like seeming and appearing are truly irrelevant when improvisation and overall design accord with one another so exactly that there is never any inconsistency between them. In such a context, belief is so lived-in that artlessness and art become the same.

My account may make the book sound inhuman, even priggish perhaps, and that would be a pity, because it is anything but. There is a sly love of foolery shared by both Swami and disciple. They *both* have something of the "play-actor" to them, and enjoy instructing by means of joke and surprise. And like that of actors on a stage, their calculation of effect does not therefore mean that they are any the less honest.

There is a short passage which may be said to indirectly propose the "poetics" of the narrative. The Swami says, after meeting a notoriously promiscuous friend of the author, "What a good man!" Isherwood is at first surprised, but then explains: "When Swami called [him] 'good,' the word had to be understood in relation to his statement: 'Purity is telling the truth.' "

The great consistency of the book, then, comes from the fact that in it truth-telling and honesty-with-oneself are not only literary values but religious ones as well. Isherwood was always good—no one has been better—at baring his own or his narrator's pretensions, for example those of vanity, cuteness, smugness, coyness. He had started doing so, searchingly and habitually, in the books of the 1930s, prompted it would seem by a predisposition that preceded his religious interests. (I think of the narrator's scathing self-analysis after his quarrel with Sally over the magazine article.) There are many examples to be found in this last book, of which one of the finest is from a diary excerpt about a visit to his friend Charles Laughton, who is dying of cancer in hospital. Laughton dozes off and Isherwood prays for him that he may have an easy death:

All mixed up with the praying, which moved me and caused me to shed tears, were the caperings of the ego, whispering, "Look, look, look at me. I'm praying for Charles Laughton!" And then the ego said, "How wonderful if he would die, quite peacefully, right now at this moment!"

It is most important not to make these confessions about the ego as if they were horrifying. They are not—and it is mere vanity to pretend that the ego doesn't come along with you every step of the way; it is there like your sinus, and its intrusions are no more shocking than sneezing.

The really important question is: Why should I pray for Charles? Shouldn't I let him do it? Wasn't I like an agent, trying to muscle in on a deal?

He never reposes in his own correctness, even in the correctness of telling the truth about his vanity. It is still necessary to ask additional questions to preserve alertness and to fend off complacency. Much of the virtue of this book emerges from such demonstrations that a ceaseless self-exposure is a religious as well as a stylistic necessity. Art and religion are not, here, separated from the main business of life. There is no clear-cut division suggested between the religious and the nonreligious, and the writer's art must be to work out ways of speaking about them that combine the utmost truth-telling with the skills of persuasion.

In spite of the importance of memoir, Isherwood was a novelist, and referred to himself as such. What does it mean, to be a novelist, when the bulk of your imaginative work consists of memoir in the form of novellas? I just said, harking back to an earlier sense of rhetoric, that he combines truth-telling with effectiveness of persuasion, but that is too general. Clearly, like any writer, Isherwood selected and emphasized in his writing so that irrelevances did not get in the way of what he saw as the historical truth (and we might remember that the young Isherwood was trained as a historian). Of *Mr. Norris Changes Trains,* for example, he tells us in his autobiography that one of the reasons the narrator is not presented as gay is that he as novelist "wanted to keep the reader's attention concentrated on Norris; therefore the Narrator had to be as unobtrusive as possible." All writers, nonfictional as well, have to do this kind of thing. The minutiae of our lives crowd in about us so thickly that we must calculate our ways of presenting what happens, or our account will stifle on its own detail. To that extent, we are all manipulators, but we may at least try to manipulate in good faith. In the event, as we have seen, the narrator of the Berlin stories ends up by becoming a fictional character, someone other than the author. For a novelist, then, the very act of selection may amount to invention. (The historian, on the other hand, cannot allow it to do that, and so in the sentence quoted above from *Christopher and His Kind* Isherwood has to explain why he made himself unobtrusive.)

There are certain specific problems for the novelist with religion on his mind, which may be described in general terms as having to do with the expression of the inexpressible. Isherwood wrote two articles on the subject, both collected in the posthumous volume, *The Wishing Tree*. In the more interesting of them, "The Problem of the Religious Novel," he proposes a fiction about the life of a saint, the greater part of which would deal with the progress toward sainthood.

> True, the path of the spiritual aspirant is hard. The mortification of the ego is tedious and painful. But I see no reason for the author to sentimentalize his hero's sufferings or to allow him to indulge in self-pity. Sportswriters find no pathos in the hardships of a boxer's training.

A true novel, then, may be based on the specific incidents of the aspirant's struggles, but the portrait of the perfected saint at the end would be pretty well impossible to do. "The mystical experience itself can never be described." Of course, a traditional method of handling it in poetry has been to treat the union with God through sexual metaphor (Crashaw, St. John of the Cross), but that will hardly work in the kind of realistic novel Isherwood is describing. The closest he ever came to it was in *A Meeting by the River,* but there he stopped well short of the sainthood itself.

Nevertheless, his beliefs were bound to affect his fiction, and I should be more specific about the problems he was up against. The central one here has to do with the fact that the very stuff of novels is that life of attachments which the religious person must ultimately view as bondage. It is that life—the life of the greedy individualistic identity (Sally, Fabrice, Maisie, Emma Woodhouse)—which prevents it from perceiving the *Atman* (the divine nature in other humans), which perception may in turn lead it to the *Brahman* (godhead). In transcendence, even in the promise of it, the novelist risks rejecting all the wonderful specifics of the narrative in which value must, in fictional terms, find its source and make its home.

Isherwood was the ideal writer to present with such a problem, given his relentless honesty and his divided allegiances. In *My Guru and His Disciple,* Gerald Heard says to him with a certain distaste, "What a *grip* on life you've got!," and yet the book is a record of his attempts to loosen that very grip. The four novellas in which he deals in some way or other with his Vedantist beliefs are, in chronological order, *Prater Violet,* "Paul" from *Down There on a Visit, A Single Man,* and *A Meeting by the River.*

The blurb I quoted, from the 1945 edition of *Prater Violet,* claims that, for all the author's intriguing transformation, "in his new novel . . . there is no trace of mysticism." This statement must certainly have reassured the potential reader's alarm lest his light reading be violated by an idea, but in fact the concluding pages of the book, in which we come to the night walk with Bergmann, describe a perception of the divine presence in fully Vedantist terms. It is a great piece of writing, never far from narrative and at the same time never far from exposition. This is the way it starts to combine the two:

> The King's Road was wet-black, and deserted as the moon. . . .
> The little houses had shut their doors against all strangers and were still, waiting for dawn, bad news and the milk. There was nobody about. Not even a policeman. Not even a cat.
>
>   It was that hour of the night at which man's ego almost sleeps.

The last statement springs from the locale, describing the ego on the point of joining the other absences: inhabitants, policemen, cats. It initiates a process of mind toward which the whole book has led, too long to quote here, which ends five pages later with "He was my father. I was his son." Out of context, no doubt, the eight words look like mere sentimental assertion, but they have been so carefully worked into, step by step, that they are deeply meaningful, moving, and convincing. Identity is in fact transcended, and what he recognizes in Bergmann, what Bergmann recognizes in him, is the *Atman*. Yet the process is presented without the use of the word, and it is an integral part of the story as story.

Vedanta and the social life of colony and monastery are directly described in "Paul" and *A Meeting by the River*, yet I do not find either work a complete success. The attempt in both cases is admirable, yet my assent is not granted in fictional terms. In the former I simply don't find myself convinced by the character of Paul, the highest paid male whore in the world, who loses interest in the things of the world: either too much or too little is attempted with him. Does he briefly achieve spiritual insight? Who can tell? He has a blank at the center, which might be everything or might be nothing. Blanks have no place in novels. . . . And the resolution of *A Meeting by the River* is achieved through a vision, or a dream, by which Ollie and his brother are brought close. Whereas the closeness between Bergmann and the narrator in *Prater Violet* was effected by a series of closely linked realizations, this one comes from what amounts to an authorial intervention, a *Swami ex machina*.

But *A Single Man* is another matter altogether. The project of the book is similar to that of *Ulysses*, though its total length cannot amount to that of a single chapter in Joyce's book: to take us through a man's day, omitting nothing in it, not even defecation or masturbation. This man was born in England but lives in Southern California, like Isherwood himself, and teaches at a college much like Los Angeles State, where Isherwood had recently taught. At times resembling "a withered boy," he is fifty-eight, about the author's age when he wrote it, and is obsessed with the signs of aging and of approaching death. Not because he is gay (though he is), but because he lives alone, his lover being dead. He literally embodies that legal term, "a single man."

On the first page, we are aware of an odd authorial tone. The mechanics of waking are described with quasi-scientific detachment. The body is presented as a mechanism ("meanwhile the cortex, that grim disciplinarian, has taken its place at the central controls"), but at the same time in a voice of wondering if knowing detachment: how curious and how interesting this specimen is, it seems to say, and though one may know all about the way it works, how unexpected its reactions sometimes are. Finally the processes of waking are completed, and the voice is less that of scientific enquirer than of science fiction writer: "It knows its name. It is called George."

This absorbed but disinterested observer now gives way for most of the book to an account of George's consciousness, which it records impartially as it follows him through his day. The economy of the book is such that each scene is essential to our picture of George. The concluding sequence of chapters, which he spends in the company of a young and attractive student, Kenny, is done with especial energy and delicacy. The writing has never been cleaner or more eloquent. The day ends with George in drunken sleep, alone, as he has started it, with no male Molly Bloom beside him.

It is at this point that Isherwood calls on his old talent for analogy. Some rock pools on the coast are described: "each pool is separate and different, and you can, if you are fanciful, give them names, such as George, Charlotte, Kenny, Mrs. Strunk." If you are fanciful: he makes the comparison and at the same time evades responsibility for it. Nevertheless, it has been made. The pool and the human identity are each a temporary organization, which by being sequestered for a while resembles a permanent structure of essential attributes. But then the tide comes in:

> Over George and the others in sleep come the waters of that other ocean—that consciousness which is no one in particular but which contains everyone and everything, past, present and future, and extends unbroken beyond the uttermost stars.

(By such words people describe God.)

We may surely suppose that, in the darkness of the full flood, some of these creatures are lifted from their pools to drift far out over the deep waters. . . . Can they tell us, in any manner, about their journey? Is there, indeed, anything for them to tell—except that the waters of the ocean are not really other than the waters of the pool?

It is the achievement of the authorial voice in this book that it can accommodate without inconsistency the tones of the reflecting essayist, the scientific observer, and the omniscient narrator as unashamedly Thackerayan puppet-master. In the last of these he goes on to present a hypothesis: "Just let us suppose, however. . . ." What if George dies in his sleep? Again he disclaims responsibility; we are free to "suppose" that George does or George doesn't, but since the hypothesis (like the analogy earlier) has been suggested, it is *there*, on the page, and brings home to us with all the more force that *if it be not now, yet it will come.*

The death is described in the original scientific tone:

Throttled out of its oxygen, the heart clenches and stops. The lungs go dead, their power line cut. All over the body, the arterials contract.

Bit by bit we watch the body close down.

And if some part of the nonentity we called George has indeed been absent at this moment of terminal shock, away out there on the deep waters, then it will return to find itself homeless. For it can associate no longer with what lies here, unsnoring, on the bed. This is now cousin to the garbage in the container on the back porch. Both will have to be carted away and disposed of, before too long.

These are the last words of the book, fierce, factual, and yet speculative. What I have to stress yet again is the sheer tact with which the authorial voice has insinuated its analogy and its hypothesis. "Unsnoring" is a word that tells us physically what might be there by its very negation; "associate" quietly and accurately suggests a connection far looser than we regularly assume for the elements of human identity. The effect of it all is double: we are both less and greater than we thought. We are less because we are, after all, mere mechanisms, and because we are just like rock pools, separate collections of loosely *associated* characteristics; but we are greater because the very looseness of the association makes us the more readily part of the infinite consciousness of God. Identity is transcended, as it was in *Prater Violet,* but here far more thoroughly and less comfortingly. The last sentence consists of a firm statement barely softened by the minuscule modification, rhythmical and syntactical, of the final three words—it is bleak indeed. The whole of the book's ending is all the more of a rhetorical triumph in that Isherwood has been enabled by his analogy to make his point about the relation between the individual and God in an entirely unreligious context, and without faltering in the consistency of his fictional terms. No *deus ex machina* here. George has returned to the great ocean as Isherwood the man has by now. It is a Vedantist emphasis, the main emphasis of the whole book too, made with an exquisite delicacy and in no way that alters the narrative conventions already established.

Everything that Isherwood wrote is worth reading, but *Goodbye to Berlin* and *A Single Man* are the two works which will clearly endure, all the more because they tied into the detail of their own eras. It is surely of permanent interest that reading them we may imagine exactly what it was like to live in the Berlin of the early 1930s or the Los Angeles of the early 1960s. The books are perhaps alike in all their unlikeness through the two principal characters, assemblages of consciousness not completely at home in their respective locations—expatriates who are of an environment and yet at the same time interestingly separated from it. They take nothing for granted: because they are not where they were born and raised, though they have made it their home, they observe it with a fiercer poignancy, they are all the more sharply aware that we are not the same as our attachments.

On a Drying Hill

Yvor Winters

Yvor Winters met me at the Southern Pacific railway depot in
Palo Alto on a hot, dry afternoon in early September of 1954.
He took me to the room he had obtained for me, where I left
my luggage, and then drove me, by way of the Stanford campus, to his home, where I was to have dinner with him, a
dinner he would make himself, as he was alone there that day
with his young son, Danny.

I had been crossing the country by train for the last few
days, and had got little sleep. I was there to start a year as one
of the fellows in creative writing at Stanford University, where
I would be working directly under Winters. I had just turned
twenty-five, and I had published a small collection of poems a
few months before, but I was too shy to show it to Winters
until the following summer.

He knew nothing about me—and there is no reason he
should have—except for the handful of poems I had submitted in my application for the fellowship. As for me, it was not
entirely my fault that I knew almost as little about him. Neither his poetry nor his criticism would have been easy to come
by in the Britain I had just left (astonishingly little modern
American poetry had been published there at that date), and I
had read only one of his essays and none of his poems. I had
applied for the fellowship more or less blind. Donald Hall,

Reprinted from *The Occasions of Poetry,* expanded edition (San Francisco: North Point Press, 1985), and from *Southern Review* 17, no. 4
(Autumn 1981).

one of the fellows for the previous year, whom I had known in England, had encouraged me to try for it; I had wanted, chiefly, to see something of America; and all I had subsequently learned about Winters was that he had a certain reputation for ferocity, though I did not know what that reputation was based on.

I didn't find him ferocious. He drove me round the Stanford campus in his ramshackle car, briefly identifying certain buildings, and out among the Californian hills of late summer, burned down to a gold from which the heat comes at you harder it seems than it does from the sky, and finally to his home, where he made me comfortable in the yard (half-orchard, it appeared), giving me a drink and then dinner with wine; and I found him merely rather silent, a man of few words. He didn't believe in small talk, whereas I apparently did. My mind somewhat dulled by my journey, I suddenly found myself chattering into a vacancy. I felt at a disadvantage.

He was about fifty-four. He was by now a portly man, and was aware of it: against an assertion in a student's essay that the "thin men of Haddam" were thin because of their wisdom, he wrote that if that were so there was small chance of wisdom left for *him*. He wore glasses and smoked a pipe, and both of these adjuncts served to mask a face that was not in any case volatile. Pleased or displeased, he was most of the time thoughtfully of the same expression; his shabby suit, too, always had the same unpressed demeanor. Almost any photograph taken of him in his last two decades shows accurately what he looked like. It was his voice that was remarkable, though I don't think I noticed it until I started taking his classes. He never played tricks with it, and in fact he habitually used a measured tone in conversation, but it was a voice which an actor would have envied, as you noticed as soon as he started to read poetry aloud. It was deep but capable of great variety in its modulation. It has always struck me that the argument of his essay on the audible reading of poetry is a little weakened by fact that *he* could read poetry in what from anybody else would have been a monotone but from him was a controlled resonance, suggesting large emotions barely held in reserve.

I don't recollect that he read any poetry aloud that evening. After dinner and my unreciprocated attempts at polite conversation, he asked me what poets I especially liked. I said Yeats and Donne, and added Hart Crane and Robert Lowell, two recent discoveries of mine. He grunted. I wasn't able to interpret the grunt.

What followed I can now see as high comedy. Had I heard of Edward Taylor? No, I hadn't. Well, let's see what I made of this. He set before me the poem beginning "View all ye eyes above." I knew that I was not at my most observant, but I certainly wanted to oblige this mysteriously demanding man while being as honest as I could. I read it through and found it closely written. I had a general impression of something reminiscent of the English Metaphysicals, which in my exhaustion pleased me rather as a panorama of distant woodland might have done. I couldn't make out the details, that is, but I liked the familiar idea of trees. What did I think of it, he asked after a suitable lapse of time. Well, I said lamely, it seems very nice. He grunted. I was beginning to find that the grunt was an ambiguous response, not always of appreciation. Did I notice anything unusual about the third and fourth stanzas? The lines blurred: Well, no. He pointed out that the imagery of the one contradicted the imagery of the other, possibly because one of them was unintentionally preserved from an early draft. I was still a romantic, he remarked as he closed the book. The tone was not disparaging; indeed it was good-humored, but I gathered that a romantic was not what he would have chosen me to be.

He asked me if I had heard of Elizabeth Daryush. No—I searched my memory for poets I might have passed over in anthologies, the Merrill Moores, the Viola Meynells, but Elizabeth Daryush—no, I didn't think so. He presented me with another open page. Good, this poem was much shorter—a sonnet, in fact; it was called "Still Life." I read it through. I read it through again. He sucked on his pipe. The poem did seem a bit lacking in substance. Could he possibly be showing me something he *didn't* like? "I don't really see much to it," I ventured. He took that book from me and closed it too. "It is a very funny poem," he remarked with a certain solid patience.

So. It was a very funny poem. I had obviously missed something again. As he drove me back to my new bed, I couldn't help feeling that I had failed a test or two most signally. I imagine he felt I had too.

A couple of days later he held a reception for the new fellows in creative writing. I met his wife, Janet Lewis, and found her immediately appealing. I also met numerous former students and was told on at least three occasions that he was a great man, a piece of information—if that is what is was—that I felt inclined to resist.

My first reaction to Winters, then, was that I didn't know how I was going to get through a year of him. The reaction lasted until about the second or third week of classes.

The term started. It was understood that I was to take Winters's creative writing classes for credit and sit in on other courses he gave; I was also permitted to sit in on other courses in the English Department.

I had come to California armed with a bunch of conclusions that I had arrived at over the previous three or four years. They derived partly from my decade of the twentieth century, partly from my Cambridge education, and partly from my own observation and reading. Many of them implicitly contradicted one another, but I saw no need to reduce them into consistency, since I wanted above all to keep myself open to books and experience—and in particular to poetry and *its* experience—that might present something to me I had not previously envisaged. The first course of Winters's I attended, on "the criticism of poetry," was an immediate shock to my assumptions, in that he set about the systematic demolishing of my favorite twentieth-century poet, Yeats, in ruthless detail. After Yeats the chosen victim was to be Hopkins, not one of my favorite poets but one I certainly respected. A particular characteristic that he attacked in the poetry of each was that of emotion lacking adequate source or motivation in the context. I couldn't help wondering who was to be the arbiter of what was adequate.

I was angry at first and fought him bitterly. I adored Yeats and was grateful to a career which had seemed exemplary to me in showing how a spirit of romanticism could survive, self-correcting and self-nourishing, into the twentieth century. Moreover, Yeats had not been taught to me as part of any curriculum: he had my special affection because I had discovered him for myself. By way of compensation I was offered Bridges, a poet I had never bothered to examine but whom I had been taught to despise. I was sufficiently able to resist the pictorial prettiness and metrical charms of "A Passer-by" but had to admit that I was impressed by the "passionate intellectuality" of "Low Barometer" and "Eros." I was, too, introduced to the sonnets of Tuckerman, of whom I had never heard, and to a poem by George Herbert, "Church Monuments," which seemed new to me, and which I immediately agreed was as good as Winters might care to claim.

This last example somewhat shook me. I had read through Herbert's poetry more than once, but had never noticed this magnificent poem before. Why not? Why had no anthologist noticed it, either? (That it is now included in many anthologies is a direct result of Winters's influence.) Winters's answer, which I found incontrovertible, was that I had missed it because I was looking for something else, the Herbert style. The Herbert style was thought of in terms of Herbert's idiosyncratic characteristics, which reached high excellence in such poems as "The Collar" and "The Pulley." In looking primarily for the typical, I had missed the untypical, which I had to admit was perhaps the best poem of all.

Compensations, then, began to appear for the degradation of Yeats. There were also certain immediate agreements. I had long liked the Elizabethans. I knew Nashe's few poems well, Ralegh's, and even some of Greville's; Donne had been, after Shakespeare, my chief teacher. So I already shared some of Winters's tastes, and though I liked the ornate and the metaphysical I needed no persuading to also like the plain style. I had assayed sententiae in my own poetry, after all.

Bit by bit the thoroughness of his arguments and the power of his examples started to win me over to much of his thought. The arguments, however, would have been nothing without the fierce love of poetry that lived behind them. That love knew no antithesis between poetry and the workings of reason, a word he used in a larger Renaissance sense rather than in its more limited eighteenth- and nineteenth-century sense. He did not, as Troilus accuses the politic bishop Helenus of doing, merely "fur his gloves with reason": it was not a genteel defense against the discomforts of passion. If Winters found unreason either destructive or dishonest or both, he did so because he knew its power from inside (see his Conradian story "The Brink of Darkness") and he never made the mistake of dismissing it as trivial. Nor, for him, did reason and passion need to be at odds: he was no Houyhnhnm; he taught from his full experience as a poet and reader. In the poetry he most admired—by Valéry or Jonson, for example—passion and reason were strong collaborators, each partaking of the other.

He was a remarkable teacher, persistent, irreverent, and specific, pressing his arguments, sometimes with considerable humor, until they were accepted. (Questions were seldom left open.) Even though much of his teaching involved the attack on reputations that had seemed to me established forever, the attacks were made so as to emphasize and isolate the really worthwhile. Pound says: "the only way to keep the best writing in circulation . . . is by drastic separation of the best from the great mass of writing that has been long considered of value."[1] Winters must have agreed with such a statement, and for him as for Pound the negations were founded on a feeling for poetry that was jealous, uncompromising, and defensive. His practice too was "drastic." Poetry was an art toward which you had to have responsibility; and it was his sense of responsibility that excited his contempt for those he found betraying it by their slipshod writing, by their incoherent thinking, or by their use of it as an exercising ground for the ego. Poetry could be, he emphasized again and again, a more *exact* and *precise* form of writing than any other. He was fond of Pound's dictum, "Poetry should be at least as well written as prose." Above all, poetry was for him a telling of the truth. Crane's words to the Medicine-man in "The Dance"—"Lie to us"—he found especially reprehensible.

His love, his passion for poetry showed clearly enough in his classes. More than one student commented on the fact that in speaking of some poem or passage he particularly admired he was apt to use the uncharacteristic word "haunting." He used it because his mind was literally haunted by certain bits of poetry, of which the power was greater than the intelligence could practically explain. And all of his students more than once heard his voice crack with emotion while reading from other people's poetry, from the sheer wonder, it appeared, that something could be done so movingly well. (This from a man with such a declared antipathy to the histrionic.)

Most teachers and critics, even quite perceptive ones, speak about poetry in terms of its subject matter, its ideas, its "themes," and its imagery, as if it were all just a piece of condensed but tuneless prose. Winters was one of the few people I have ever come across who have spoken—spoken at all, let alone intelligibly—about the way meter works and about the way poetic movement (whether in metrical or in free verse) influences poetic meaning.[2] He would discuss, in fact, what actually happens in the sounds of some famous line in a Shakespeare sonnet, attempting perhaps for the first time to describe what has attracted generations of readers. Meter and verse movement, however, were only a small part of what he discussed. He realized that a poem is the sum of components that bear relationships of almost infinite complexity toward each of the other components; the relationships moreover are not static—they vary in relation to the other relationships; and they continue to vary as the poem moves on from line to line. He was fully aware of why it is so diffcult to talk accurately and usefully about poetic technique, and yet he found it worth the effort. But he went further: his was an examination of technique that became, ultimately, also an examination of the way in which knowledge is simultaneously discovered and transmitted.

He was not a bully, though he did not suffer fools gladly. He certainly believed he had come as close to a description of what poetry is and can be, and of the way it works, as is possible. (It is notable that the illogic of the visionary was largely excluded from that description and so was implicitly classed with the work of the charlatan or the self-deluded from which it is sometimes difficult to distinguish it.) But he proceeded largely by means of persuasion and demonstration rather than of dogmatic assertion, and though his arguments were rigorous in detail he was always prepared to discuss the views of the opposition. He respected the alert opposer more than the inert disciple. As I have said, I argued with him from the start and was always ready, often too ready, to disagree. There were times, later, when I half compared myself to the difficult army recruit in the Hollywood movie who earns the liking of the ferocious sergeant in direct proportion to his earlier recalcitrance.

When his friends and students had called him a great man, I had not realized that the word *great* was a favorite term of his. Poetry was divided into individual poems which were either great or not; by extension, their authors were also either great or not. It was a strangely loose word (surely it just meant "very good"?) for such a strict thinker. What is more, though the word would have been clear enough once you became accustomed to its application, in that it was meant to indicate a carefully assembled canon of acceptable poems, the canon became shorter as the years passed, and both individual great poems and great poets got eliminated from it. Of course, it is only human to change one's mind, but Winters's mind-changing was hard on some of those who got demoted and confusing to those who witnessed the demotions.

But this is to look ahead. In the autumn of 1954 I moved, in any case, from extreme distrust to trust, coming to realize, in sudden humility, that I had a lot to learn from the man. (Whether I came to use the word *great* of him I do not remember.) At the very least, he was introducing me to a number of good poems that I had not read, French as well as English and American, and this in itself was enough reason for gratitude. But further, he had a closely worked out conception of the way art fits into the human universe. If you are given the chance of going to school under a man possessing an extraordinary mind, who has attempted to completely assess the consequences of all his assumptions, you would be a fool not to take advantage of it, even if the risk were of ending up a slavish follower.

Perhaps it was the creative writing classes that really won me over to him. The whole notion of "creative writing" and of taking classes in it was new to me. Poetry was something that I, like all the other poets in history, had taught myself up to now. But since I had come here as a creative writing fellow, I was supposed to take the course.

The classes were tiny and informal. They took place in Winters's office, and consisted of the two current poetry fellows and any others he had found promising on the basis of work they had shown him; we were seldom more than seven in all. New poems were usually given in to him earlier in the day, and consisted of single copies which he first read aloud and then passed around the group, an awkward procedure. He would comment on the poem himself first and then the others would add their comments, and the discussion would start. It was a loose arrangement, and sometimes he would ask someone else in the group to open the discussion.

In my arrogance, I was at first astonished at the usefulness of what was said, by him especially. His insights were always useful, whether you were able to work on them or not. He had the knack—the genius perhaps—of divining your intentions, even if the poem was so obscurely or clumsily carried out that those intentions had become hidden. He habitually showed sympathy and patience. His criticism was specific and helpful; it was of the sort that went: "Well, if this part of the poem doesn't work, you could try doing such-and-such," so that if such-and-such wasn't appropriate at least your mind had started recreating something you had assumed you could do no more to.

He would sit facing us in his morris chair, gently sucking his pipe, a genial and informal teacher very little distinguishable from a friend. The informality allowed him a much greater inconsistency than he showed in the more public arena of the larger classes. He would often cite the virtues of poems by people he would seem to have largely repudiated in print— Crane, Frost, or Williams. When he became thus informal, when it came down to poetry in the process of being made, he returned to the more open mind of his youth. Discovering that

I had read nothing by Williams, he urged me to read him through as soon as possible. Once, of a poem I wrote about Merlin (we favored that kind of subject in the fifties), he remarked that, much as he liked it on the whole, it lacked in detail both Crane's sharpness of image and Cunningham's sharpness of conceptual language. Crane's line about the mammoth turtles, for instance, had remained for him a touchstone of the alive bright image through over twenty-five years. I even knew his feeling to run completely contrary to his printed statements: he once said to me of Robert Lowell something like, "Lowell *has* it, you know—for all his faults he is a poet; damn it he can write," a remark that any reader and most students of Winters will find nothing less than astonishing. It was perhaps a weakness in his method that he would have been able to find no place for it in his published criticism.

He was, above all, a brilliant teacher because of his knowledge of what is *behind* a poem, what makes a poet want to write in the first place and thus separates him from a prose-writer. It is something many critics cannot grasp, that—what?—sense of urgency and of intensity, of being possessed by the subject, however apparently quiet that subject may seem. For, as he well knew, this intensity (and he might have disliked my word) has nothing to do with melodrama or disproportion of view. He could find it even behind a short piece by Barnabe Googe or an epigram by J. V. Cunningham. They were in the plain style, yes, but they were not just rhyming prose. Thus one of his unkindest epithets was "journalistic." For him, most of Auden's later poems were simply journalistic, neither language nor rhythm raising the writing above that of superficial prose.

Two other words I remember him using to express reservations about poetry were "soft" and "gentle."[3] Not for him "the meek, the white, the gentle," but then he had no wish to be Tom o' Bedlam either. He had a predisposition on behalf of the hard, the brave, the reticent, and the stoical. Such is not really surprising if you keep his published work in mind, whether poetry or prose.

To such a man, and to such a poet—for I had soon read his collected poems—I was glad to spend a year of apprenticeship, fancying myself as the modern counterpart of some young painter in Florence apprenticed in the workshop of a master painter. Indeed Winters was a master of his workshop too: I think he saw his job in these classes as being not simply to improve the writing of various students but to help us become "great poets."

Since like many another I hoped to join the company of English (and American) poets, I certainly didn't wish to oppose him there. I hoped I was tough enough to use what he had to offer me and still where necessary resist him, that is without becoming an imitator. Many others of his students, before and after, did and were to keep their poetic identities intact—Donald Hall, Edgar Bowers, Philip Levine, Robert Pinsky, Alan Stephens, Scott Momaday, Kenneth Fields, and so on—some even coming in the end to completely reject him. But all of us learned from him, even the most reluctant.

For some of his students his formulations provided a refuge, a harmonious world where everything had already been decided in accordance with certain rules. It became a temporary or lifelong asylum for those who might otherwise have fallen into the arms of a church or a political party. The attraction lay in the logical *completeness* with which he had worked out his ideas, and such students became disciples in a literal sense, limiting themselves to another man's world; but, as my friend Ted Tayler remarked at the time, another man's world, however wonderful, is always smaller than the world you can discover for yourself. I had seen the whole thing happen before, among the students of F. R. Leavis at Cambridge. But on the whole I find Winters's disciples a much humaner and better-tempered lot than Leavis's.

It was not only the ideas of course (it never is), but also the man himself that attracted them, as he did me as well. It is no loose Freudianism to say that for many students he was a father figure. He even told me about one of them who asked his approval of a prospective suitor. He didn't relish such a role at all; it embarrassed him. One thing is certain: he was not interested in having a following, in the acquisition of power; if he had wanted power, he could easily have found some means to get it many years earlier, but it, like reputation, was of no interest to him.

The complete disinterestedness, the modesty, the lack of anything self-serving, only made his character more seductive and his personality more inadvertently charming. It is difficult to explain his diffident sweet-naturedness to those who know his personality rather through the prickly and often eccentric footnotes of *Forms of Discovery*. His manner could be, in Marianne Moore's word for it, "badgerish"; it could be brusque, intolerant, even brutal; it could also be generous, good-humored, and relaxed. His wit was quiet and disarming. But he had to feel at ease with you first.

The next summer came around, and I had finished my three terms at Stanford. Some of us asked him out to dinner, but he did not like eating out and instead he and Janet gave a party for us. He showed us his study for the first time: it was a small one-room building across his backyard, with (if I remember rightly) cheap prints of the heads of favorite writers framed on the wall, Emily Dickinson and Herman Melville guarding his desk. His prize Airedale Black Jack was in the freshly hosed-down yard, and muddied the new white ducks of Tom Arp, one of my fellow students. I felt nostalgia already. I had written of lot of poetry during the year, my range was wider, my technique sharper—I had learned so much! I had every reason to feel gratitude. On the train to Texas, where I intended to spend the following year, I drafted a poem to Winters, in which I attempted as a kind of tribute to suggest his own later style. When I came to send him the finished poem later, he merely remarked that he hoped he was worthy of it. I concluded that he didn't like it and it was not until somewhat later that Janet told me he had been pleased and touched by it. He was a shy man, and never knew quite how to receive compliments graciously.

The rest is epilogue. In 1956 I returned to Stanford to do graduate work for the next two years. Winters encouraged me to attend the creative writing classes again, and I went regularly at first, but then I started to become wary. There had been stories of students becoming so dependent on his classes that when they had ceased attending them their source of poetry had dried up altogether![4] I didn't think I was in quite such a bad way as that, but I did conclude that, as I had started writing without help, I should continue without it. I deliberately began to go more seldom and ended by not attending his classes at all.

This was formal contact. Of informal we had for a while more than before. He was, if anything, more generous of his time, his attention, his company, and his house. One Thanksgiving when everybody else was in the kitchen, we were sitting at the hearth of his front room when he announced, with much shyness, that he had lately "committed" two poems, the first in years. They were "A Dream Vision" and (probably) "Danse Macabre," both of which he thereupon recited to me. It may have been at this same time that he talked to me at some length about his parents (I had met his mother, a very old woman, on a similar occasion). I had never felt so close to him as I did that afternoon.

Another time he seriously asked my advice about giving a public reading of his poetry for the Poetry Center in San Francisco. He said that in my poem to him I suggested that he had fenced himself off from the world (it had not been my intended emphasis), and maybe he should consent, for once, to give this reading. I had never heard him give a full formal reading of his work, except on the Library of Congress record, so I encouraged him to do so, as much for the sake of his audience as for himself, and he did indeed give it.

I think it was on my return to Stanford from Texas in 1956 that he asked me to call him by his first name, Arthur. I was moved by the gesture, but on thinking about it was a little depressed. As Allen Tate said to me many years later, when I once met him briefly, "Winters made the mistake of judging people by their poetry." I already knew this; and what was more I knew that my poetry would sooner or later disappoint Winters. He would feel affection for me only as long as he could approve of my poetry and my ideas. So to take up this token of increased intimacy had its ironical aspect. I felt as if I were a partner in some doomed love affair from a French novel: I could see an end in sight even while we achieved the point of greatest symbolic attachment.

I left Stanford eventually without a degree, bored and exasperated with graduate work that seemed to have nothing to do with the reasons I had taken up English in the first place; but of course I continued to visit and write Winters: I kept up with him, though he never liked any poetry I wrote after 1958, the year I left. Once in the sixties when I sent him a group of poems, he wrote back that they were simply journalistic and maybe I should try to learn how to write prose instead. The letter came as no unexpected blow. I had been anticipating something like it for years, and I wasn't going to fight him about it. If he had a streak of brutality in him, I had a streak of sentimentality.

My relationship with him since his death has developed and changed, as my relationships do with the dead. I can see now that in his criticism of me he pinpointed a certain irresponsibility, a looseness, a lack of principle—a promiscuous love of experience, perhaps—which I know I need to keep going, lacking his theoretic firmness. He had been right that first evening: I am still a romantic, thinking with Keats that "nothing ever becomes real till it is experienced—Even a Proverb is no proverb till your Life has illustrated it." Winters rather could believe with Ben Jonson that

> Not to know vice at all, and keepe true state,
> Is vertue, and not Fate;

that one can evaluate and make choices without physically engaging the actions that one comes to reject; and that the romantic immersion in the life of the senses moreover tends to destroy the power of discrimination, and therefore is to be avoided. (If I appear to be confusing the imaginative with the moral life here, I do so because for Winters at their acutest they were the same thing—the good poem makes moral discriminations.) It is perhaps an argument between two temperaments. I say temperaments because an Olympian wisdom would take neither side: you cannot possibly be "virtuous" (or a good poet) without a degree of undiscriminated experience. On the other hand, a life that was all experience and nothing else would simply wear out the body and the head. The question of *how much* experience to have is one to be judged as you go along; it is a matter of improvisation. What complicates the matter, also, is that experience is always lived for its own sake, not with one eye cocked on its possible usefulness for moral or poetic ends.

Perhaps in this last paragraph I am trying to be the victor in our implicit argument, or perhaps I am being as fair as I can be. I am not sure. Certainly I have peculiar difficulty in recording these memories of Arthur Winters, partly because my recollections of him are jostled and in danger of being replaced by the voice of the books (though I have deliberately avoided referring to them while I write), partly because the man's very forcefulness still arouses my defenses, and partly also because of the disconcerting oppositions between the rigor of his critical presence and what I could almost call the tenderness of his private presence. I have, however, a clear picture of him securely in my mind, which I will keep there till the end. Rather than a single memory, it is probably a composite made from a series of memories. We are sitting in his front room or on seats under the trees, drinking wine and talking; he sucks on his pipe during repeated silences; but he speaks at times, measuring what he says—he speaks of poetry with a peculiar intimacy and dedication for the art about which he had more to tell than anyone else I have known.

NOTES

1. Ezra Pound, *ABC of Reading* (New York: New Directions, 1960), p. 13. Somebody could write an interesting essay about the effect of Pound's early criticism on Winters both early and late. By the 1950s Winters had long repudiated Pound's ideas and practice, though he continued to praise certain poems (with reservations) and continued to quote from the early criticism. But Pound's taste had influenced his own youthful taste, and the coincidence of many of their favorite poems was frequent. Both singled out, for example, Mark Alexander Boyd's "Fra wood to wood," both admired Crabbe, both admired the early Elizbethans (though with a difference of

emphasis), both praised Landor, both expressed contempt for the Romantic poets (with a slight occasional exception made for Keats), and both had little time for the famous eighteenth-century poets. Pound too must have been an influence in encouraging by his example both the iconoclasm and the personal search for "the best poems" in the face of the accepted anthology pieces. (I suspect that Pound too had almost as great a dislike for the middle and late Yeats as Winters did.) Since the labors of both Pound and Winters have, ironically, enlarged the canon of those anthology pieces in the last few decades, the similarities of taste between the two men may seem less striking now than they did in the 1950s.

2. It is worth noting that Brooks and Warren incorporated the gist of the third section of Winters's essay "The Influence of Meter on Poetic Convention" in the third edition of their textbook, *Understanding Poetry*, without any acknowledgement that I can find. That is, they acknowledge their quotation of one of his own poems with his own markings of the stressed syllables, but they do not acknowledge that they have borrowed his theory of the scansion of free verse as well.

3. I think it was Alan Stephens who pointed this out to him in a class.

4. This makes Winters sound like an addicting drug. But dependence on a strong-minded teacher is one of the greatest dangers to originality in a creative writing class. The opposite danger is the overpermissive teacher: his class sits around liking each other so much that they start to write poetry that aims at pleasing all the other students. Such writing-by-consensus produces the "well-made poems" of our day, homogenized, fashionable, and vapid. (I teach the subject myself nowadays, and have made myself aware of the dangers.)

Two Saturday Nights
Rewriting a Poem

This is the story of how I took fifteen years to write a poem.

In 1975 I was reading the *Divine Comedy* in the course of a three-year attempt to grasp it as people do who have little Italian, a bit of Latin, and much French. I think that must be the way the young Eliot read it—out of the Temple Classics edition of around 1900, taking it Canto by Canto, first reading the English literal prose translation and then piecing together the Italian on the opposite page, reading it aloud as best I could, and taking it slowly, but at worst getting closer to it than if I had read it in the verse translations of Carey and Binyon. However far I may have been from *really* reading Dante, I certainly arrived at a sense of that extraordinary compression which must be one of the sources of his power.

I loved besides the combination of the cerebral with the visionary in a man whose ability, whose necessity, was to speculate about his own ranging imagination. And I was, not for the first time, much attracted by the tune of terza rima, a form with great potential for speed and condensation and inconclusiveness: when I think of Dante's verse form I get the image of a big dog running fast, its body packed with meat and muscle and import.

It was at this time that I wrote a poem about the Barracks, one of the most famous, one of the most lurid indeed, of the bathhouses in San Francisco during the 1970s. (It was the only

Reprinted from *COS Equals SinOverTan/SinOverTan* 1 (1991).

one I ever heard of that was raided, not by the vice, but by the narcotics squad.)

Saturday Night

I prowl the labyrinthine corridors
 And have a sense of being underground
As in a mine . . . dim light, the many floors,
 The bays, the heat, the tape's explosive sound.
People still entering, though it is 3 A.M.,
 Stripping at lockers and, with a towel tied round,
Stepping out hot for love or stratagem,
 Pausing at thresholds (newness never ends),
Peering at others, as others peer at them
 Like people in shelters searching for their friends
Among the group come newest from the street.
 And in each room a different scene attends.
In one, three portly men, each bare in his seat,
 Passing a joint between them, as polite
As if at home in civilized retreat.
 Next door, packed twining limbs seem in half-light
Continuous flesh unjoined to head or foot.
 Next, one lies patient on his belly all night,
His special interest reared and resolute.
 And here one waiting as his trip comes on
Stares at the handcuffs which his friend has put
 Open before him, but his friend is gone.

I'm still on top of it, but only just.
 Not hell, not even a phenomenon.
And yet tonight I'm full of self-mistrust . . .
 Then one whose very eyes brightly conspire
Moves from the mob and touches me. Clear lust—
 I suddenly flare up—fire in the mine, all fire!
It burns down to the self, the baths, the night,
 Which grant me thus a great and good desire.
I think, at least for now, it's all all right.

I never published this poem because something dissatisfied me about it, as if I hadn't quite told the truth in it. For all the qualifications he makes, its author seems limited and complacent. "Look, I scored!" he says with the defiance of an insecure stockbroker. Harold Norse once wrote a poem about a housepainter on his lunch break: virile and juicy, he sits relaxed in the sunshine with white paint still flecking his eyelashes; and first of all the poem asks us to admire him from a distance—it is a beautiful moment, perhaps *because* of the distance. (D. H. Lawrence would have had him rightly warning the greedy: NOLI ME TANGERE.) But then the poet, apparently, comes up and propositions him, because they have sex somewhere and the poem subsides into a mere boastfulness. I hate that kind of poem, but it was what I had written here.

In 1975 I had recently been granted a new subject matter, one which would have been unpublishable probably ten years before and certainly twenty years before. It was still the time of Gay Liberation, a phrase which now has a quaint but worthy ring to it. There was talk of a "gay community," something I doubted existed. But community it was, as Ellen Willis described it, in the course of a fine article in the *Village Voice* (Jan. 24, 1989):

> The lesbian movement of the '70s was not primarily about liberating desire . . . but about extending female solidarity; for the gay male community solidarity was, at its core, about desire.

That's what we were a part of, a visionary carnal politics. No wonder Blake was often cited!

Something more. The 1970s were the time, as I heard someone say later, of a great hedonistic experiment. And the word experiment inevitably recalls to me the way people spoke for years about Soviet Russia. In the early 1940s, when I was at boarding school because of the Blitz, my mother wrote to me on the invasion of Russia: "Does this mean that the great experiment will fail?" (She was ignorant of Stalin's massacres.) And visionaries are much the same, whether they are political or religious or sexual. As hippies were the indirect heirs of the communists between World Wars, so we were the direct heirs of the hippies, drug-visionaries also. At the baths, or in less organized activity, there was a shared sense of adventure, thrilling, hilarious, *experimental*. In our deliberately distorted vision, we crossed gulfs as dramatic and enormous as those in John Martin's landscapes, on the huge pinions of our sexual momentum. We tried to make the ecstatic commonplace, each night of it a building block for an apocalyptic Holy City—a City of Eros.

> There are many different varieties of New Jerusalem,
> Political, pharmaceutical—I've visited most of them.
> But of all the embodiments ever built, I'd only return to one,
> For the sexual New Jerusalem was by far the greatest fun.

That was a spin-off of 1990. I wanted it to resemble the epigraphs to Kipling's stories. It was designed as an introduction to the poem I did eventually come to write at this time, which I don't think is much like Kipling in itself. I tried yet again because I thought some poet should do something about a great imaginative experience—the excitements and intensities of a bathhouse, with the druggy fantasy always bordering on the dangerous. I kept the first eleven lines from my old poem but after that I had to rethink the whole thing. This time, fifteen years after I had started it, it necessarily became a historical poem:

Saturday Night

> I prowl the labyrinthine corridors
>   And have a sense of being underground
> As in a mine . . . dim light, the many floors,
>   The bays, the heat, the tape's explosive sound.
> People still entering, though it is 3 A.M.,
>   Stripping at lockers and, with a towel tied round,
> Stepping out hot for love or stratagem,
>   Pausing at thresholds (wonder never ends),
> Peering at others, as others peer at them
>   Like people in shelters searching for their friends
> Among the group come newest from the street.
>   And in each room a different scene attends:
> Friends by the bedful lounging on one sheet,
>   Playing cards, smoking, while the drugs come on,
> Or watching the foot-traffic on the beat,
>   Ready for every fresh phenomenon.

This was the Barracks, this the divine rage
   In 1975, that time is gone.
All here, of any looks, of any age,
   Will get whatever they are looking for,
Or something close, the rapture they engage
   Renewable each night.
                              If, furthermore,
Our Dionysian experiment
   To build a city never dared before
Dies without reaching to its full extent,
   At least in the endeavor we translate
Our common ecstasy to a brief ascent
   Of the complete, grasped, paradisal state
Against the wisdom pointing us away.

   What hopeless hopefulness. I watch, I wait—
The embraces slip, and nothing seems to stay
   In our community of the carnal heart.
Some lose conviction in mid-arc of play,
   Their skin turns numb, they dress and will depart:
The perfect body, lingering on goodbyes,
   Cannot find strength now for another start.
Dealers move in, and murmuring advertise
   Drugs from each doorway with a business frown.
Mattresses lose their springs. Beds crack, capsize,
   And spill their occupants on the floor to drown.
Walls darken with the mold, or is it rash?
   At length the baths catch fire and then burn down,
And blackened beams dam up the bays of ash.

An Anglo-American Poet

Interview with Jim Powell

Do you have a sense of an English audience for your work, or a sense of two audiences, English and American?

Audience has always been a difficult question for me. It's the last thing I think about. People used to ask did I feel I was an English poet or an American poet and I would always be wishy-washy about it. Then a few years ago I came across a reference to myself as an Anglo-American poet and I thought, "Yes, that's what I am. I'm an Anglo-American poet." So that resolves that question! I don't think of the audiences as being that different. What people say about me, and it's probably true, is that in many of my poems I write about an American subject matter in an English way, by which they mean metrical and in rhyme—which may be an English way, though it's been used by some Americans. Of course free verse is not particularly English; very few English people have written decent free verse. One of the few is Lawrence.

Bunting, too.

Bunting, if you call that free verse. But it's such a tightly disciplined free verse, it keeps on moving into something very like meter.

Reprinted from *PN Review* 70 (1989). The interview took place in my office on the campus of the University of California at Berkeley on May 8, 1989. Special thanks to Karen Bondaruk, who transcribed the tapes.

Can you give us a history of your relation with the possibilities of form? I know you started out working in traditional meters.

I started out writing in meter because that was the way everybody around me was writing. In the late 1940s the poets I admired wrote in meter; there were a few English people who were writing sloppy free verse but I didn't pay much mind to them. And then when I started publishing I found myself identified with some people who eventually became classed as the Movement. However, my contention is that the Movement didn't really exist: what we had in common was a period style. I'm pretty sure I'm right because people not included in the Movement wrote in the same style. Then in 1954 I came to America and was able to read many of the modernists I'd never come across before—people like Stevens and Williams. And I read Pound for the first time with understanding. I immediately saw a great deal of potential in free verse but I wasn't able to write it at once because after you've been writing metrically for some years, you have that tune going in your head and you can't get rid of it or when you try you write chopped up prose. My way of teaching myself to write free verse was to work with syllabics. They aren't very interesting in themselves. They're really there for the sake of the writer rather than the reader. But they were a way of getting iambics out of my ears. Around the time of *My Sad Captains* I wrote about thirty poems in syllabics but I haven't worked with them since about 1964. I bother to say this because some people are under the impression that I am still writing them because they don't count and they don't know the difference between free verse and syllabics. But as a discipline syllabics did succeed in teaching me what free verse I'm able to write, which the English don't think is very good.

I don't think they can hear free verse, actually.

I don't think they can hear it either. But that's something else again, isn't it. Now I write a mixture of the two. I have a phase writing free verse, then a phase writing metrical verse, rather than both at once. As you know, I've been writing metrical verse pretty much exclusively in the last few years—though the poems I published in a pamphlet called *Undesirables* are in free verse. I chose to publish that booklet in England.

Just to irritate them?

Just to irritate them! And it did irritate some of them very much, I must say! There was one person who thought I was imitating Williams! [laughter] Whatever else I was doing wrong, I wasn't imitating Williams. I always hoped that my experiences with free verse would enrich my metrical verse as well. And vice versa, of course. At one time I hoped that I could combine the virtues of free verse with those of metric— which is a little like the alchemists' search for the philosophers' stone. I don't think it's possible, though Bunting comes as close as anybody. I'm not able to do it anyway. I've always counted on having a modern life span—unlike people who died in their twenties or thirties in Elizabethan times—

Marlowe knifed in a bar fight . . .

—or like the Romantics who drowned or had tuberculosis. Luckily I was right. I'm going to be sixty this year. And I didn't want to be one of those poets who do their best work when they're younger. I counted on learning things as I went along. I always figured that there was going to be time for everything, that I had time to try something like syllabics even though it might turn out to be a dead end, because I might still learn things from it.

Bunting says somewhere that Yeats would often have a poem on his desk for nine months (though he might also be working on a half dozen at once).

Writing a poem can take any length of time at all. It's happened to me very occasionally that I've written a poem almost in one draft. And sometimes I have worked on poems for a year or so—I don't mean continuously, but you know, you try again. One of the poems I finished fairly recently, a very simple poem called "Nasturtium," I wrote in one version that I didn't like at all and I just kept a few lines of it and wrote a completely different poem. I'm pleased with it now but it took me, for such a simple, small poem, it took me a hell of a long time—something like three years, off and on.

Still, your poems in traditional forms, the poems in cross-rhymed pentameter quatrains and in pentameter couplets in your forthcoming book, The Man with Night Sweats, *for instance, often convince me that you can think in rhyme, that you are completely at home there and can move naturally inside those forms.*

I suppose there are times when it's easy and so you could say that I'm moving comfortably within the form, but those times are extremely rare. What I find more to the point is that in looking for a rhyme, or in trying to get a meter right, you are often having to go deeper into your subject so that you discover things about it, and about your reaction to it, that you didn't know before. You are digging in—because you have to. In looking for a rhyme, even just in mechanically trying all the consonants in turn on your suffix, you are exploring possibilities in your subject: how can this word be applied to my subject, how can that one? As you get more desperate, you actually start to think more deeply about the subject in hand, so that rhyme turns out to be a method of thematic exploration.

Who were your poetic heroes as a teenager? Who were you mad about at fourteen?

Oh, I was mad about Keats and Marlowe when I was fourteen.

What Marlowe?

The plays. It wasn't until much later that I read *Hero and Leander,* which I now find as good as anything by Marlowe, possibly better than the plays. It seems to me exquisitely funny, and vigorous. It has a kind of freshness that reminds me of Spenser, but Spenser never gets it quite so well. He is so intensely decorative that he doesn't have quite the guts that

Marlowe has. It's immensely erotic but in a very unsmutty way. It's delightful. It's what Keats was trying for, but Keats never quite got it, I think because he never had the erotic experience to back it up. But *Hero and Leander* is one of the top poems for me. Even Shakespeare didn't get quite that quality. He did better in many ways of course but I don't think that he got that particular erotic delight in things that Marlowe has. It's a delight so great that he can laugh at it in the middle of it. He kind of giggles with pleasure. It's so wonderfully heterosexual. It strikes me he's not making any distinctions between the heterosexual and the homosexual in the poem. That's another thing I find very pleasant.

In my teens, I wanted to be a novelist. I read so many Victorian novels that later when I did my undergraduate work I didn't need to read any more to answer the novel questions on the exams. I wanted to be a novelist very much in the Victorian sense: I've always been interested in characters. In my last book I did actually start a series of character studies—it's called "Transients and Residents." At one time I envisaged this as being rather ambitious, maybe as many as twenty poems, each one dealing with somebody I know. There's one poem in the new book, "Looks," that could well be a part of it.

Then toward the end of my teens I really started to admire Auden a great deal. Early Auden. Anne Ridler said that reading Auden made her want to write poetry in the first place. He had an idiom that seemed to be adapted to anything he did and to be able to link the ancient craft of poetry with modern experience. You must remember that I was young and ignorant and I didn't know about the modernists, and I didn't know much about Eliot then and I hadn't read Baudelaire, or I would have known that other people had written about modern experience. But Auden seemed so available. He made writing seem easy. I am very grateful to him for having, in one sense, started me off. I did feel a great need to disown him, as one does with one's earliest influences, as soon as I started to write a little more seriously. You know, it's called castrating one's father.

Once I got to Cambridge around about the end of my first

year I and my friends discovered Yeats together for ourselves. The most extraordinary thing about Yeats is that he was not in the curriculum. His last *Collected Poems* had not yet come out; he'd been out of print the whole of the war and after the war and it was about 1952 that the *Collected Poems* finally came out and we all bought copies. It was extraordinary because we'd always understood that Eliot was the king of the world, that Eliot was *the* modern poet. There was no possible rival, and suddenly here was somebody as good or better, it seemed to us, someone with a lot more vigor, a bigger range, and more exciting. And we discovered him for ourselves, which was a wonderful thing to be able to do with a major poet, because every other major poet by that time has been presented to you as part of a curriculum.

When did you start reading Baudelaire?

I started reading Baudelaire actually just after I finished national service and before I went to Cambridge as an undergraduate. Baudelaire has meant a tremendous amount to me over the years as somebody to be learned from—as much as anybody apart from Shakespeare, perhaps. I reread him last year and realized that a lot of the poems I'd been writing were aspiring, though not consciously, to something he achieves in many of his late poems—poem like "Les Sept Vieillards" and "Les Petites Vieilles" and "Le Cygne." That's the kind of poem I most want to write.

Clive Wilmer gives me the impression that for many readers in Britain right now you are a California poet—something at least as exotic as Baudelaire. [laughter]

The English think of California as being a good deal more exotic than it really is. The English by and large don't seem to think that people lead regular, normal lives in California. I lead a very mundane, ordinary life here. It's true I'm queer, but you can be queer in England, too, you know. But I don't lead an exotic life and the kind of experience that I write about is not exotic. I've written a lot recently about people dying of AIDS but they're doing that in huge numbers in Europe now also. And death has always been quite prevalent. But I detect a feeling of resentment in such comments. There were several resentments apparent in England against my last book. One was that much of it was in free verse. Another was that much of it was about gay life. But there was an underlying and implicit resentment that I was a Californian now, so I was altogether a creature of artifice.

When we were talking about doing this interview you said you weren't sure you wanted to examine your processes of composition too closely. Why?

Superstition? I'm always amazed that I can write a poem. I've been writing them since I was eighteen or so but I'm always amazed that I can write a poem I can read through and think it's ok and worth publishing. There are times when I can versify and versify very boringly and I don't know why that isn't so all the time. I don't know what gives it that extra energy or where it comes from when it comes. Someone who was interviewing me the other day for *Gay Times* in England, Alan Sinfield, was saying that he views me as a traditional poet—and he didn't mean anything bad by it! [laughter]—a traditional poet because what I seem to be doing in the structure of the poem is bringing new experience to something I know already and putting the two in combination. This is what one does in the traditional poem. One brings the new experience to the traditional form. This is turn makes me wonder what connection all this has with the structure of the Horatian ode. The really noticeable thing I've found in my reading of Horace's poems has been that so often what he seems to be doing is putting together two brilliant, unfinished poems, on the same or similar themes, but coming from different directions and somehow resolving them by bringing them together—or not resolving, quite, but he brings about an ending by combining the two. Horace is wonderfully experimental in the structure of his poems and that excites me a good deal—experimental in a way that Baudelaire isn't, that Donne isn't. Baudelaire sticks to the subject, usually, and Donne always sticks to the subject, or goes deeper into it or finds analogies for it. He doesn't change the subject as Horace does. So comparatively speaking Horace is extraordinarily bold.

Who do you read with interest among more recent poets?

Bunting seems to me the most interesting poet in Britain since the death of Yeats. That's not such an odd statement to make. A lot of people agree with it. The trouble is the English are hung up on Larkin. Larkin was a poet of minute ambitions who carried them out exquisitely. But he really isn't a very important poet and right now he exercises a terrible influence on English poetry because if you admire somebody like that so much it means you're not going to be aiming very high. His distrust of rhetoric was also a distrust of feeling, a distrust of daring. Certainly he was right to be distrustful of rhetoric, but on the other hand I would sooner read poets who are able to take those risks. He himself was a very good poet, though a very bad tempered one, I think. I like Robert Pinsky's word for him: "sour." And this has got in the way of Bunting's achievement, which is insufficiently admired in Britain and certainly insufficiently admired here. Bunting seems to me one of the great poets of the century in the English language. He's difficult, but then lots of people are difficult, and working through the difficulties is in itself rewarding. He's the most rewarding poet that I've come across in the last ten years. Bunting is able to use modernism in a way that should be exemplary for all of us. He's able to use it in relation to his origins, in relation to tradition. He is able to combine the influence of Pound and Wordsworth—something that Pound never envisaged. Somebody who's able to do that is able to do the whole thing, and *Briggflatts* is one of the great poems of the century. I wouldn't qualify that at all. It is one of the few great poems of the century. It seems to me greater every time I read it.

Mina Loy is somebody I wasn't able to read until much later than I wanted to. I was very impressed by what Winters and Rexroth and Pound said about her, but for a long time only a small part of her work was available. Then Jargon published

Roger Conover's edition a few years ago so I was finally able to read her complete poetry. I wrote about her recently in an essay named "Three Hard Women" that appeared last year in a *festschrift* for Donald Davie called *On Modern Poetry*. It fascinates me that other people obviously don't like her. Now she's available, but she's still not included in any of the anthologies of poetry, even of women's poetry where often a lot of extremely inferior poets are included. And she's got it. Her best poem is "Der Blinde Junge" but many of her early poems are absolutely brilliant. But they are clever, and they are unkind, and they are difficult—and people don't like that. They love H.D., who for me is largely a crashingly boring poet but people love her because they see her as some kind of earth mother or because she's a lesbian. She didn't like sex and she didn't like herself, whereas Mina Loy adored men, liked sex, she's a very sexual writer in a wonderful way and she's hard, and she's unkind and she's funny. I would love to have met Mina Loy. She is one of the few poets I would really like to have met at her height. She must have been a great deal of fun to be around.

I was rereading Robert Duncan recently because I wrote that article about him, and so I decided I was going to read all his major work again. The two volumes of *Ground Work* have hardly hit the public consciousness yet, apart from people like ourselves who were already his readers. You wouldn't know that those two books have come out, and yet they're magnificent. They're a great crown to a career. I suppose that in about fifty years time everybody will agree with us, but it's a bore waiting for posterity to catch up with one's views. We were very different poets. Duncan had a program of being avant-garde and romantic and my program is entirely different insofar as it's a program. He was a wonderful man to be around, and his conversation was terribly brilliant and exciting. Having lunch with him, I would go back and write down all sorts of ideas in my notebook that I'd never had before. God knows he was a learned man, probably the most learned man I've ever known. It was partly a disorganized learning, but it was not so disorganized as it seemed.

It wasn't disorganized: it just violated most of the boundaries of received organization.

He didn't believe in the canon. He thought that the canon had to be constantly violated and that is what more recent criticism has been starting to say. I have thought this for some time. I suppose I really started to think about it when I knew Winters, and because Winters was constantly saying that the canon wasn't enough, that there were all these poems, and he'd specify them, that were good, and yet they weren't in the canon and people didn't read them. I'm against the idea of there being a fixed canon, though I often teach as though there were one, because there are certain good poems, famous poems that students ought to know about.

In America recently literary journalists have begun to talk about something they call New Formalism.

I have very little interest in any literary movement of the last forty years. The two current literary movements in this country are the New Formalism and the Language Poets. Neither interests me. I'm interested in individual poets, not in poetics. Poetics is such a big word nowadays, such a fashionable word. Every now and again I ask myself whether I have any poetic theory. I suppose somebody could assemble one for me simply on the basis of my practice. I think it would be full of inconsistencies—which perhaps it's just as well I keep unexamined. I'm interested in writing poetry and I'm genuinely not very interested in the theory of poetry. The New Formalism troubles me partly because, there, people might tend to identify me as one of its precursors. I'm not interested in encouraging such a school, because I think they should also be learning from people like Bunting and Pound and the other modernists.

It's a pretty narrow tradition they're committed to drawing on.

Yes, it's far too narrow a tradition. They should be reading Ginsberg. In fact, one of them wrote me and asked if I'd contribute to his magazine. I said "No, I'm not interested in reading the people that you suggest printing (he'd given me a list); I've just written an article praising Ginsberg and I think you should be reading him instead." And I do think that somebody like that should be reading Ginsberg, and someone who writes like Ginsberg should also be reading poets like Robert Herrick. It works both ways. We should all be fertilizing each other. It's not particularly profitable at this time to be separating ourselves into armed camps. There's not enough talent to go around. Maybe a tradition that's able to take account of the avant-garde and of the traditional is necessary. That's what was so wonderful about Duncan. He was able to absorb all kinds of influence, even someone as foreign to the avant-garde traditions he started from as Ben Jonson—in that wonderful sequence the "Seventeenth Century Suite" in *Ground Work: Before The War*.

Yes, there are passages, too where you'll hear heroic couplets embedded in his most avant-garde-appearing poems.

Or as he once pointed out you'll sometimes find lines Edna St. Vincent Millay could have written—and he said "that's the kind of risk I *know* I'm taking." I loved that kind of defiance in him. Anyway I don't think I'm particularly against schools as such, though they have bored me during my lifetime. But I thing that they are only useful when there is a central monolithic tradition that is worth opposing. And we don't have such a central tradition now. We have fashion, but that's not the same thing at all. Another problem with theory is it's simply boring.

When is your next book going to come out and why are you delaying it? I know it's basically done and has been for more than six months now.

Yes, I finished *The Man with Night Sweats* last August and plan to have it come out in 1992. The reason I decided to wait is quite simply that after I publish a book I have trouble starting composing poetry again. After my last book it was about two years, and after the book before that it was about two and a half years. I simply got stuck and couldn't seem to write anything. So I thought I'd play a game with this and see if it worked. Since the periods not writing seem to be connected with the idea of closing off some whole area of experience in publishing a book, I thought that perhaps this time if I simply put the book in a drawer for a few years I could perhaps go on writing. And I have, indeed, gone on writing. I don't feel I have any reputation to keep up. I don't care about that, keeping the eye of the public. I'm too old to bother about that kind of thing any longer.

Some of the strongest poems in The Man with Night Sweats *are about friends you've lost to the AIDS epidemic.*

Yes. It seems to me that one of my subjects is friendship, the value of friendship. It is a subject that has preoccupied me in recent years. This shows especially in *The Passages of Joy,* though nobody noticed it. Everybody noticed the gay poetry, but there are many poems about friendship in that book and a great many more in a new one that have to do with friendship, or imply it as a value, as indeed it is for me. And if you're a writer and you have a lot of friends who suddenly die, then you're going to want to write about it. And then, one of the oldest subjects is how you face the end. One thing I've been greatly struck by in the people I've watched die is the extraordinary bravery with which people face death. So many of one's values—for humanist atheists like myself, as opposed to religious people—arise in confrontation with death.

Are you an atheist who admits the supernatural?

Yes, that's a good description of me. It's like Bunting—Jonathan Williams refers to Bunting as "my atheist Quaker friend."

I asked Pinsky what he thought I should ask you and he said he wanted to know why you appear to be so calm at the heart of the maelstrom. [laughter]

What maelstrom? I'm a cheerful and rather superficial person most of the time. I simply don't notice things, so when I seem to be calm and stoical maybe it's because I didn't notice them.

You're just oblivious? [laughter]

I'm just oblivious, right. You know, people are so nice, they often don't credit me with a normal degree of stupidity or with a certain lack of observativeness. . . . I'm such an associationist talker, I must not be a very good person to interview.

But then we get to play with the transcript.

Play with it as much as you want my friend. [laughter] Mina Loy is my mother, you'll end by having me say.

There, that's an idea.